MOMENTS OF GRACE

STORIES OF ORDINARY PEOPLE
AND AN EXTRAORDINARY GOD

MOMENTS

OF GRACE

NANCY JO
SULLIVAN

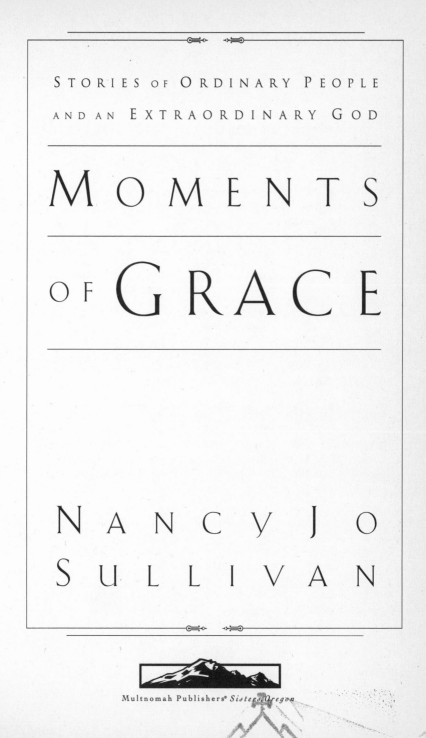

Multnomah Publishers® *Sisters, Oregon*

MOMENTS OF GRACE
published by Multnomah Publishers, Inc.

© 2000 Nancy Jo Sullivan
International Standard Book Number: 1-57673-698-9

Cover image by Photodisc
Design by the Office of Bill Chiravalle

Scripture quotations are from:
The Holy Bible, New International Version © 1973, 1978, 1984
by International Bible Society, used by permission of
Zondervan Publishing House. All rights reserved.

Also quoted:
Holy Bible, New Living Translation (NLT) © 1996. Used by permission of
Tyndale House Publishers, Inc.

Please see the back of this book for a listing of permission for
several of the stories.

Multnomah is a trademark of Multnomah Publishers, Inc.,
and is registered in the U.S. Patent and Trademark Office.
The colophon is a trademark of Multnomah Publishers, Inc.

Printed in the United States of America

For information:
MULTNOMAH PUBLISHERS, INC.
POST OFFICE BOX 1720
SISTERS, OREGON 97759

Library of Congress Cataloging–in–Publication Data
Sullivan, Nancy Jo, 1956–
Moments of grace : stories of ordinary people and an extraordinary God /
by Nancy Jo Sullivan.
    p.cm.   ISBN 1-57673-698-9
    1. Grace of life (Theology) 2. Christian life. 3. Conduct of life. I. Title
BT761.2.S92 2000   242–dc21   00-008963

00 01 02 03 04 05 — 10 9 8 7 6 5 4 3 2 1 0

In praise of family

CONTENTS

ACKNOWLEDGMENTS

I wish to extend my thanks to the following people—

To my family: Your encouragement and supportive presence have sustained me throughout the literary project. Because of you, my life has been blessed with many undeserved moments of grace.

To my editor, Nancy Thompson: Most of the hard work of editing was done through long distance phone calls. Week after week, Nancy and I worked together as a team, sifting through drafts, deleting paragraphs, and correcting punctuation. Sometimes as we reshaped stories, we came upon sentences that made us laugh so hard that we had to take a five-minute phone break. Other times, we reread paragraphs that evoked emotions of sadness; we got used to pausing for tears. One afternoon as we brainstormed for a book title, Nancy crunched on pretzels and I downed half a bag of licorice. "Stress food," we decided. Nancy, thanks for sharing your editorial expertise, for bringing life to mediocre stories, and for being a friend.

To my friends at Multnomah: Bill Jensen. I'm grateful for the lunch you bought me last summer. I apologize for eating only one bite—I was so excited that you thought I could write a book.

Alice Gray. You've always been my best cheerleader. When you told me I was a gifted writer, I started believing I was.

Cliff Boersma. I appreciate the time you took to walk me through the contract.

Steve Curley. Hey, buddy! We came up with a title after all.

To all my friends at *Guideposts* magazine, especially Rick Hamlin, senior editor: Thanks, Rick, for launching me into my writing career. Over the last five years, you, more than anyone, have helped me to "get to the point."

To lifelong friends who remain true: Marion and Roxanne, Karen, Sharon, and Deb. I love you always.

INTRODUCTION

M y father taught me how to tell a good story.
Every morning when I was a little girl, I would get up early—way before my eight other siblings—and clad in a red-checked bathrobe, I would make my way to the kitchen and join my dad at the table.

Coffee percolated in an orange plug-in pot. A wall clock ticked softly and a bowl of Rice Krispies waited only for their slosh of milk to start a-crackling.

Dad was a big man—broad-shouldered and thick at the middle. A former navy officer, Dad was not only very strict but ran a tight ship of our eleven-member family: daily scrutiny of our rooms, rations on Oreo cookies, line-up shoe shine inspections before Sunday church.

It was in these early morning minutes that I saw a different side of him.

"Good morning to the beautiful Cochise," Dad would say, the inflections in his voice rising and falling like he was reciting a poem.

Dad pronounced my nickname "Ko-Cheeze." Dad's version had it that Cochise was an Indian princess who lived in the 1800s, dwelling along the Mississippi River with her family. Later in life, I would learn that Cochise was in fact a highly respected Indian chief who led the Apache nation.

No matter. Dad's made-up adventures of the mythical maiden brought unforgettable enchantment to my childhood.

When I was in kindergarten, Dad talked of "Baby Cochise."

"She was born at harvesttime, when the night moon was orange and the sky was filled with diamond stars…" Dad began.

He spoke of a small papoose that Cochise slept in "a secure little pouch made of leather and feathers and beads." During the first days of Cochise's life, her father, "Big Chief," would suspend her papoose from the boughs of ancient trees, and go about his own work nearby. All the while he watched the cradle board sway in the autumn breeze.

"Did Cochise cry?" I asked. At that time, my colicky baby sister Annie wailed all the time.

"Not much…it was too peaceful." He closed his eyes and sighed. I was sure he could see the serene scene.

On the morning of my ninth birthday, Dad told me about a tribal birthday ceremony held in honor of Cochise's birthday. I was captivated as he tapped his hands on the kitchen table imitating the beat of the drum.

"What did she wear?" I asked, eager for more details.

"She wore beaded moccasins and a buckskin skirt with fringe. Around her neck was a silver necklace with turquoise stones. Her flaxen hair was braided," came the description.

As I grew Cochise grew too. When I was twelve, Dad portrayed a preteen Cochise who sounded a lot like me.

"She was fiercely independent," he told me one morning.

Often Cochise would canoe down the waters of the Mississippi. Dad described thick forests that framed the waterfront. There were cicadas and leaping deer. "A ruby-throated hummingbird reserved her sweetest song for Cochise," Dad said.

I could almost hear the waves slapping against the boat as Dad told about Cochise's adventures fishing for walleyes or searching for precious jewels and shells along the shore. And I could almost smell the forest pine, the fragrance of the wild roses, and the musty leaves.

"Cochise loved all that God created," Dad explained.

I heard one last story of Cochise on the morning of my wedding.

"She wore a ceremonial robe that sparkled with white beads. There was a wreath of wildflowers in her hair," Dad said. "Big Chief found it hard to let her go."

Now so many years later, I dwell with my own family just about a mile away from the Mississippi River. I often think of Cochise as I drive along the meandering waterfront.

Of course, she is not real. Still, I imagine her canoe and hear the lapping of the waves. I can almost smell the forest scents of her childhood. And I listen for the sweet song of the ruby-throated hummingbird.

Though Dad died over a decade ago, these images continue to inspire me. As a Christian writer, I find myself searching the "shoreline" of my life for the jewel of a good story. When I find one, I ask God my Father to join me at the kitchen table of my heart. There, the two of us bring meaning to true life moments.

Bless me with the warm breezes of inspiration; let this story be filled with the fragrance of Your presence; plant Your word in me that I might share it with others.

COFFEENS

One of my favorite Scripture passages is: "I have called you by name, you are mine" (Isaiah 43:1). I like this verse because it suggests that our names are extremely important to God and that we are known by Him as friends. Even very special friends.

I had spent most of the week on the couch, sick with a winter flu. Though my husband and kids offered their sympathy, they were busy with commitments—my husband with his teaching job and my kids with school and sports.

The daily household routines had basically broken down. There were eight loads of wash stacked in the laundry room, the dirty dishes were piled in the sink, and the carpet looked like it hadn't been vacuumed in days. The kids were going on their third night in a row of pizza.

After days of huddling under a quilt, sipping cups of Thera-Flu, and watching reruns of Matlock, I could not take another morning in the house. I needed to get out. I was tired of being isolated from the world.

As I bundled up in sweaters and scarves, I drove a few blocks to Coffeens, a coffee shop at the edge of our town.

Shivering my way through the snow-speckled wind, I opened the front door of the shop, a jingling door chime announcing my arrival.

"Hi, Nancy. We've missed you," Donna, the owner, said as I entered. Just hearing the sound of my name brought unexpected comfort. It really felt good that someone had noticed my absence.

A fellow mom and friend, Donna stood behind the counter dressed in a yellow apron and a pair of blue jeans. She was making a latte for a student with a backpack.

I was a regular customer at Coffeens. I loved smelling the herb teas and imported coffee and fresh-baked pastries. I loved the familiarity of the painting of Henry Coffeen hanging on the wall, next to a shelf of potted plants. Henry was Donna's great-great-grandfather. He was the founder of Watertown, New York, in the year 1800. I often laughed at the artist's portrayal of Henry. He was wearing a coonskin cap that reminded me of Daniel Boone.

"I've been sick," I told her. As I went on and on, dramatizing my aches and pains, Donna nodded her head.

"A few weeks back, I had it too. It's a nasty virus, isn't it?" she replied.

Two elderly men listened from a nearby table. They were drinking coffee and playing cribbage. Regulars too, they always wore flannel shirts and Dockers.

"Honey and hot water," one of the men called out to us.

"It'll cure what ails ya," added the other.

Donna took a ceramic mug from the shelf above the coffee pot, a shiny yellow cup decorated with orange slices. It was my favorite.

Filling the mug with hot water and a little chunk of lemon, my regular drink of choice, she waved a jar of honey in front of me. "Wanna try it?"

"Sure," I sniffled, glad for the collective interest in my recovery.

As I sat down at a small table by a sunny window, a heavy-set woman nodded to me. She was doing needlepoint as she lounged on an antique couch that Donna had picked up at an estate sale.

"Hot orange juice," she said as she pulled a needle through her fabric. "My grandmother's cure from way back."

"I'll have to try that."

The rising steam from my cup warmed my face.

A man wearing a fireman's uniform scoured the newspaper at an adjacent table. He took one last gulp of coffee as his beeper went off.

"Keep sittin' by that window," he advised as he waved good-bye. "When you're sick, sunlight is a good source of vitamin D."

The wind chimes from the door jingled as Jill, a good friend of mine, walked into the shop. In between coughs, she waved hello to me while Donna fixed her the hot water-honey remedy.

"I've been on the couch all week," Jill said as she made her way to my table.

"Sick?" I asked.

We laughed as we exchanged a list of identical symptoms. "You should see my house. It's a disaster," I told Jill.

When Donna heard our chuckles, she drew near with a plate of just-toasted bread. For the rest of the morning, the three of us shared the casual conversation of small-town friends.

We talked of the basketball game our kids had won, the winter sale at the shoe store down the street, the storm that was coming at the end of the week.

Every now and then, the men playing cribbage would add a thought or two: "Better get your snowblowers tuned up," they advised.

I started to feel a little better.

It wasn't just the hot water and honey. It was the comfort of being part of a community, the healing of hearing my name after days of isolation, the solace of drinking a cure that some-one had prepared especially for me.

Later that morning as I arrived home, I felt a newfound surge of energy.

Though I still wasn't completely well, I was happy to be up, doing a little housework and making soup for dinner. It almost felt like I had been resurrected from the dead.

"Maybe Coffeens is a hint of heaven," I told myself.

I imagined a far away coffee shop set on the edge of eternity. Someday I would arrive at that heavenly door, a golden chime announcing my entry.

"Hi, Nancy. We've missed you," God would say.

With good friends gathered around a sunlit table, I would drink the warm healing water of God's mercy.

I would eat the homemade bread of eternal life.

I would laugh away the "ailings" of life—my body and mind forever whole and healed. *That would be wonderful,* I thought.

The kids barreled in through the front door, tossing their backpacks in the entryway and breaking into my thoughts.

"Mommy…you look better," my youngest daughter said, hugging me.

The other two smiled knowingly: "I bet she went to Coffeens…"

A MAILBOX MERCY

*When I reflect on the incident in this story, I am reminded
of a passage from Shakespeare that is among my favorites:
"The quality of mercy is not strained, it droppeth to the
ground as a gentle rain from heaven upon the place
beneath; it is twice blessed. It blesseth him that gives and
him that takes."*

I t was two days before Valentine's Day. I was mad at my
mom. Though it had been weeks since the argument, a silly
argument, I still found myself brooding.

"Why should I be the one to apologize?" I told myself as I
signed my name to a valentine I had bought out of obligation.

"No 'I love yous' from me," I said as I smacked a stamp on
the red envelope.

A little later, I drove to the post office. The pink shadows of
a February sunset danced off office buildings and ice-spotted
roadways. I steered my van into a line of cars waiting at the
drop-in mailbox.

Minutes passed. The post office traffic remained at a stand-
still. Rolling down my van window to see what was going on, I
noticed a rusted station wagon at the front of the car line.

Is the car stalled at the mailbox? I wondered.

A woman in a Ford Taurus the color of cherries became
impatient with the wait. She honked at the station wagon,
loudly, holding her horn down for several seconds at a time.

An elderly man hobbled from the rusted sedan, his face

looked dazed. It was clear that the horn had startled him. Holding a cane to balance his uneven gait, he shuffled to the mailbox, clutching a stack of red-enveloped valentines.

"I'm sorry," he called out to the woman, his voice soft and trembling.

The woman opened her car door and walked with quick steps to the old man's side. Wearing a pink blazer and a thick gold necklace, she threw her arms around his shoulders.

"*I'm* sorry," I heard her say.

In the last sunlit rays of the day, the man gently patted her on the back, resting one hand on his cane.

I watched through my windshield as these two strangers enacted a passage from the Bible that I had long since committed to memory: "If you forgive those who sin against you, your heavenly Father will forgive you" (Matthew 6:14, NLT).

I felt ashamed as I realized I had been harboring unforgiveness in my heart, waiting for my mother to apologize.

While honking the "horn" of my anger, I had placed all the blame for the argument on my mom, refusing to acknowledge the hurtful words I had spoken to her.

I needed to ask for her forgiveness.

I also needed to offer her the same kind of mercy I had just witnessed at the mailbox, the unwavering mercy of God.

As the old man and the well-dressed woman parted, the line of cars began to move in a steady pace toward the mailbox.

With one hand on the steering wheel, I carefully reopened my mother's card.

Now one car away from the drop box, I quickly rewrote my Valentine's greeting:

"I'm sorry. I love you, Mom."

The Broken Ballerina

I have found that faith is a dance that can only be mastered through time.

S ilent Night" played from a low-volumed radio in the kitchen. It was midnight, just a week before Christmas. Outside our suburban home a blizzard raged. But set against the colonial panes of our living room window, a glistening Christmas tree lit the bitter night with glittery silver tinsel and strands of tiny white lights.

My husband and three children were upstairs, fast asleep. I snuggled into an armchair near the tree as I savored the late night silence of my home.

It felt good to relax. That morning the kids had gotten up at 6:30 to decorate for the holidays. Most of our Christmas ornaments now hung in clusters on the tree, sideways and backwards and upside down. But I liked the way it looked. *It's custom decorated,* I thought.

As I began to doze, I heard the sound of soft, slippered footsteps coming down the stairs. I turned to find Sarah, my Down's syndrome daughter, standing on the landing. Dressed in a teddy bear print robe, she held a small cedar box, latched with gold hinges.

"M-M-Mommy...we f-forgot s-s-something today."

Though Sarah had just turned fourteen, she still bore a childlike sweetness. With a dimpled grin and curled ponytails, her hazel green eyes sparkled through pink-framed glasses.

"You remembered," I said, as she nestled in next to me, setting the box on my lap. Together we opened it.

Inside were keepsakes I had saved since her birth: stacks of greeting cards, letters yellowed with age, baby photos of unforgettable days. Sarah ran her hand over a child's baseball mitt and a tiny pair of dancing slippers. Then she found what she was looking for, wrapped in tissue—a Christmas ornament, a tiny ballerina fashioned from delicate wood. I had bought it for her years earlier, just hours before she was born.

Once this ornament was a symbol of dreams surrendered; now it evoked images of a spiritual journey filled with tender, irrepressible lessons of faith.

As Sarah laid her head on my shoulder, I took the ornament into my hand and thought about the day that journey began.

In my mind, I traveled back in time to when I was a little girl. It was early Christmas morning, and it was snowing outside the small Lake Superior home where my family lived.

As I tiptoed down our stairway, I saw my dad piling presents underneath the Christmas tree in our living room. He motioned me near. As I settled into his lap, he handed me a small package wrapped in shiny red foil.

Carefully ripping away the wrapping, I found to my delight a music box—royal blue and trimmed with colored spangles.

I opened it. From a mirrored ledge within, a ballerina, small and delicate, sprang up, her pink leotard glittering with ivory sequins, her lace net skirt gathered into a silver sash around her waist.

I watched in wonder as my father wound the box with a golden key. With each crank, the ballerina began to twirl round and round to a tune that sounded like clock chimes. Enchanted, I dreamed that one day I would be a dancer too. But it was not to be.

More mental snapshots appeared in my mind's eye: the day my parents told me they couldn't afford dance lessons; the night I watched a middle-school friend perform in a recital that I wanted to be part of; the morning I learned that I had not made the final cut for our high school dance line. I even remembered a ballroom dance class I had taken in college. By that time I had learned to laugh my way through ungraceful glides and unmastered steps. At last it seemed I had dismissed the dancing visions of my youth.

But a few years later, on a sunny July morning, it seemed those snuffed out dreams were beginning to rekindle.

That was the morning my husband Don and I arrived for an appointment at the obstetrics clinic. We were newlyweds and I was pregnant with our first child; our doctor had ordered a routine sonogram.

While we watched the movements of our unborn baby on the ultrasound monitor, we were utterly amazed. Our child seemed completely and impeccably formed, even though I was barely showing. As we ran our fingers along the screen, we traced the outline of a baby's hand, counting each finger. There was no sign or suspicion of a disability, only the steady sound of a strong heartbeat reverberating through the room.

"Looks like a girl," the doctor said. He had made the discovery incidentally, but for us it was a moment of tender, unexpected awareness. This was our daughter. She was real. We would name her Sarah Marie, which means "God's princess."

In the months that followed, we made preparations to welcome her. Though we weren't making much money as first-year schoolteachers, we had enough in savings for a down payment on our first home; a vintage Cape Cod with paint-worn window boxes and siding that needed repair.

With the extra funds Don earned as a baseball coach, we bought a new crib and redecorated the baby's room. While Don painted the walls, I stenciled dancing bears along the windowsills and sewed ruffled curtains from pink and white gingham.

As the summer wore on, my waistline expanded and I resigned myself to a wardrobe of plaid maternity tops and stretch-paneled pants. It seemed as if I grew bigger by the day, and Don and I bantered on and on about our baby.

Who would she grow up to be? A renowned surgeon? A famous musician? A bestselling author?

"She'll be the next Babe Ruth," Don teased as he came home one autumn day holding a toddler's baseball mitt. He had paid a quarter for it at a garage sale.

"She will dance," I replied with a smile, reminding him that I had more sophisticated plans for Sarah. "She will dance…" I whispered the words every time I felt the kicks and turns of my baby. Even late at night when I couldn't sleep, I envisioned the glittery costumes she would wear and the soft-ribboned slippers that would hang from a peg in her room. As I imagined her bowing in a circle of stage light, I prayed that God would bless the hopes I held.

Then, on a blustery November afternoon, when the first snow of the season fell, it seemed that God was gently affirming my prayers.

I had been Christmas shopping at the mall. Passing store after store, I watched as merchants donned display windows with colored lights and red-berried garlands. Inside one shop, I saw a twelve-foot Balsam fir adorned with hundreds of decorations. I decided to buy an ornament for the baby I would be cradling by Christmas.

From houses to hockey sticks to cookies and crayons, that tree held every ornament imaginable: beeswax candles, cinnamoned hearts, brown furry bears, angels, and stars.

As I reached to take a closer look at a red-ribboned stroller, I accidentally knocked a small ornament from the bottom branch onto the floor. Kneeling down, I picked up a tiny ballerina.

Her creator had crafted her simply with a white-painted

face, two dotted eyes of blue, and a penciled line of red for a smile. She wore only a sleeveless smock trimmed with a lace ruffle, no sequins or sashes or slippers. Yet her form was elegant, almost regal, with arms arched upward in a pose that looked like praise.

I wondered if God was speaking to me. Perhaps this ornament was a sign from heaven, a divine reassurance that all my childhood dreams would one day be redeemed in the dance of my daughter.

I handed the clerk a ten-dollar bill as she wrapped the ballerina in layers of gold tissue paper.

Suddenly, I felt pain. The initial stages of labor had arrived; I knew it intuitively. Hurriedly I zipped the ornament into my purse.

Later that night, at 9:46 P.M., Sarah Marie was born. Another forty-five minutes and we heard a knock on our recovery room door. My baseball-capped husband answered with Sarah tucked in his arms. It was our doctor.

"I'm sorry," he said in almost a whisper.

Still clad in his surgical blues, he sat down on a chair next to my bed. He clutched a clipboard scrawled with the notes of an undeniable diagnosis.

"We think your daughter has a genetic abnormality." He spoke of symptoms—flaccid muscles, delayed reactions, an extra chromosome.

"I believe she has Down's syndrome," he said softly.

Don took off his cap and hung his head. I squeezed his hand. We had made plans and dreamed dreams for a child much different than the one he was describing.

"There are support groups here at the hospital for parents of the handicapped," the doctor continued. As he handed us brochures and suggested resources, I quietly repeated the words: "Parents of the handicapped." It was an identity that demanded a surrendering of dreams.

I wanted to deny his findings. I wanted to say, "Recheck her; there's been a mistake; she's fine." But somehow I knew that the diagnosis was true and that our lives had changed forever.

Midnight came. Late shift nurses set up an overnight cot for Don, right next to my bed. As I held Sarah in my arms, the lights in the maternity ward were dimmed and Don fell asleep.

In the faint glow of a bedside nightlight, I looked in wonder at her newborn face. I searched for signs of a disability, but all I could find was the loveliness of a little girl. For her eyelashes were long and curled, her skin was soft and blushed, and her left cheek was sweetly dimpled.

"My little ballerina," I said softly.

With misting eyes, I reached for my leather bag. Unzipping it, I searched for a Kleenex, but wedged between my wallet and car keys I found instead the tissue-wrapped ornament.

I lifted the covered keepsake into my hand and peeled away each layer of wrapping.

The ballerina was broken.

"M-M-Mommy" Sarah said as she nudged my arm, prying me away from the memories I had filed under "unforgettable."

"L-L-Look," she said.

I watched as my daughter sifted through old childhood photos; snapshots of Sarah riding a bike or chasing a butterfly or throwing a baseball to Don. Every picture had captured her smiling. Throughout the years, the challenges of her disability had been overshadowed by the immeasurable joy she had brought to our lives.

"M-My f-f-favorite," Sarah said as she held a photo I had taken just a few weeks earlier; a picture of Sarah standing on stage in a glittery dance costume.

For the last decade, Sarah had taken dance lessons at a studio called "Uniquely Able." She had learned how to dance, and our family had attended every recital.

As I looked at the photo, it occurred to me that Sarah had taught me the dance of faith.

Because of her, I had learned how to hold onto the hand of God; the strong steady hand that guides us through our unexpected losses, the gentle hand which lovingly twirls us to the other side of our broken dreams.

On that other side I had discovered, much to my delight, the irrepressible blessings of surrender and acceptance; I had uncovered the wondrous plan of God.

As I closed the lid on the cedar box, I placed the ballerina ornament in Sarah's hand.

"Go ahead," I said, motioning for Sarah to hang the ornament on our tree. Every holiday, this was her honored task.

As she ran her hands over the glue that had long since dried over the wood of the ballerina's arm, her eyes sparkled with happiness.

"She's not broken anymore," Sarah said.

Together, the two of us placed the ballerina on the highest branch of the tree, instead of a star.

"Not anymore," I said.

HOCKEY MOM

Sometimes it's the smallest deeds that make the biggest difference.

In Minnesota, hockey is competitive, even at the youngest age.

Maybe that's why I felt panicky as I drove my nine-year-old Rachael to the local hockey team try-outs. My palms were sweating and I kept tapping my fingers on the steering wheel.

"Daddy's the only one who can lace my skates," she said. Her voice was higher pitched than usual. Dressed in padded equipment and a yellow helmet, Rachael was ready for this important afternoon practice. Today she would skate in front of a panel of coaches—today the "little girls" team would be chosen.

"You know Dad had a late meeting," I said as we pulled into the parking lot of the indoor arena.

I tried not to sound worried, but it was my husband who always took Rachael to practice; he had mastered the art of tying her skates tightly. I hadn't.

Though I had grown up just a few blocks from an ice rink and I had learned how to pull laces through the lightweight leather of a figure skate, hockey skates were different. They were made of black inflexible fabric and lined with rigid layers of padding. It took brute strength to tie a hockey skate; I had always left that up to Don.

As I grabbed Rachael's stick out of the trunk, the two of us made our way past the ice rink toward a chilly dressing room framed with concrete and benches.

Inside the room, parents in down jackets tied their daughters' skates as they knelt on a padded floor. Not one spoke. As breath after breath froze into a white mist, not even one person made eye contact. The tryouts were triggering a collective tension; I could feel it.

Rachael found an empty bench, unzipped her workout bag, and pulled out a pair of newly sharpened skates.

"Mommy, you don't know how to tie them," she reminded me again in a whisper, so no one could hear.

"Trust me," I said softly as I looked around the room. I was hoping to meet the gaze of a kind face, someone, anyone who might give me a quick lesson in lacing.

"No one's gonna help us," my daughter said.

"It can't be that hard," I replied.

Kneeling down, I took Rachael's left skate and began to pull a thick waxy shoestring through fourteen hard metal eyelets. My hands began to stiffen from the chill and Rachael's skates were still cold from the car. It was hard to grip and tug.

Though I strained to bind each skate with a secure knot, the final crisscrossed ties remained loose and droopy. When Rachael stood up, her skate blades buckled and her ankles wobbled. Behind her helmet, I could see my little girl's eyes filling with tears.

"They're not tight enough," she cried quietly.

A long-haired woman in a red wool headband looked up from a nearby bench. She had just finished lacing the last loop of her daughter's skate. When she saw Rachael's tears, she glanced at me, her eyes full of heartfelt understanding.

"First time lacing?" she asked.

"First time," I replied.

As she motioned Rachael to sit down next to her, the woman knelt and began to retie my daughter's right skate.

"It's all in the knuckles," the mother advised as she showed me how to stretch and pull and loop each lace, eyelet by eyelet, one at a time. I looked on, studying each quick grip and grasp.

"Always doubletie them," she added.

As the mother secured one last knot, Rachael stood up and smiled, a mouth guard trimming her grin. With her laces now taut, her ankles were tightly braced. I applauded as she proudly hobbled her way out of the door and onto the rink for tryouts.

"Thanks," I told the mother who had come to our aid.

"You're very welcome," she replied. "Now your daughter will skate her best," she added.

I watched from the bleachers and my eyes followed Rachael as she glided effortlessly on shiny blades over a glasslike rink.

While a panel of clipboarded coaches graded her skating skills, I looked across the bleachers and saw the mother in the red headband. She was cheering her daughter on. She looked over in my direction. As we waved to each other, I prayed that God would reward her for her kindness; she deserved a blessing.

I thought about her unselfishness. She could have deliberately ignored our need, choosing instead, to give her child an edge over mine. Instead she took a moment to notice a demoralized mom, a tearful little girl, and a pair of poorly tied skates.

Her good deed reminded me of Jesus' words: "Do unto others as you would have them do unto you."

I was reminded that we are called to reach out to others and that even a small gesture of compassion has the power to alter the course of someone's day.

Later that afternoon, as Rachael and I drove home from tryouts, the two of us couldn't stop talking about the mom who had rescued us from a hockey heartache.

"Can you imagine what would have happened if she hadn't helped us?" I asked.

Rachael's eyes grew big as she shook her head in dismay. Then she smiled.

"Her daughter made the team," Rachael said.

I was glad; maybe this was the blessing I had prayed for.

"Good deeds go a long way," I told Rachael.

"I know, Mommy," she replied. "And I made the team too!"

IN THE WAITING ROOM

I think hospitals are holy places. When people are faced with sickness and suffering, they often think about God. I know I did when our baby underwent life-threatening heart surgery. Day after day I asked my Creator: "How can you allow such pain?" One morning as I sat in the hospital lobby, God sent someone to help me answer that question.

ifteen years ago I often asked the question, Why does God allow suffering? I had just become a new mother, but my baby daughter was sick, very sick. Not only did she have Down's syndrome but the doctors had discovered a serious heart defect. Six weeks after Sarah's birth she had surgery, and for days my husband and I kept vigil by her bedside in intensive care.

Behind swinging steel doors marked in red letters Sterilized Area, our baby lay in a corner crib. Huddling over her bed, we held her tiny hands and listened to the beat of her heart as thin jagged lines on the monitor above etched her progress. Nurses adjusted her breathing tubes and changed her bandages while doctors murmured softly and wrote notes on clipboards. They said her prognosis was grim.

Sometimes it was all too much, and I needed to get away from the sterile syringes and the pulsing of electrocardiographs. Each day I slipped down the hall to a lobby lined with chairs. There I turned the pages of outdated magazines or watched talk shows as I chewed on leathery apples from the vending machine.

Other parents sat there too, parents like us, parents whose children suffered from heart disease or cancer or ailments so rare I had never heard of them. As I listened to their stories, I wondered how God could allow such disappointment and pain.

Then one day a new face arrived, a tall bearded man holding the hand of his five-year-old son. He wore the distinctive dark clothing of an Orthodox Jew: a tall dark hat with a brim, a long coal-colored coat with tails, and black tapered trousers. Curious, I watched as he placed a shawl and a small black prayer book on his son's lap. Then he looked up and gave me a quick nod in greeting.

His name was Shimon. A rabbi, he had flown in from Boston that morning and would be staying with a nearby Jewish community. His son needed a new kidney. As the days passed, Shimon turned that lobby into a sort of living room. He set a gold-framed picture of his family on a table next to the vending machine. Each day he offered me kosher food from a paper bag: fresh-baked bread, red grapes, seasoned fish. And every morning he put on the shawl and his yarmulke, then with his prayer book opened he recited several Hebrew prayers in a soft voice.

Whenever he prayed I watched something amazing. One by one, each parent turned away from magazines and candy bars and talk shows. Together we bowed our heads. I don't think any of us knew or fully understood his prayers. Most of us had come from Christian traditions, yet each of us felt a certain strength, a quiet comfort as he prayed.

In between those prayers and the breaking of bread, Shimon and I made conversation. We talked of the cold Midwestern winters, the ocean breezes in Boston, our families, and God. He spoke of the great I Am, an inextinguishable fire that led his people out of darkness, a brilliant flame that blazed in times of uncertainty. He was at peace with God. I, on the other hand, was not.

Then early one Sunday morning, Sarah took a turn for the worse. The doctors discovered a staph infection in her blood. It could take her life. My husband and I stood vigil by her crib. She lay almost lifeless, her small body bruised from weeks of incisions, needles, and stitches. Like the other children in that ward, she had battled more disease in a few short weeks than most people do in a lifetime.

As I held her tiny ashen hand, I retreated to a dark, despairing place where the light of faith is snuffed out and God's absence seems real. Then I made my way to the lobby and buried my head in my hands.

"Can I help you?" I heard the rabbi ask.

After a long silence, I finally looked up. "Shimon," I asked, "why does God allow such great suffering?"

For a moment Shimon bowed his head. Then he turned to me and said something I will never forget. "I do not know much about the God you hold in your heart," he began, "except that He suffered and died on a cross. Perhaps it is your suffering God who draws near to you now."

As he spoke, images of Calvary began to fill my mind: the somber sky, the nails of iron, the cross itself. In my mind I drew near to that cross. I could feel a wounded Christ wrap His injured arms around me, my sick baby, my husband, Shimon, and every parent in that lobby. An anguished God aching with the anguish of His children.

Soon a warmth began to fill me. It started out as an ember of hope, then became a blaze of faith. God was present. I knew it. I felt it.

Three days later Sarah recovered from the infection that had threatened her life. With suitcases packed to leave the hospital, we passed through the lobby one last time. Cradling my baby, I searched for Shimon to say good-bye. He wasn't there. Some of the other parents happily reported that a kidney had been found for Shimon's son, so Shimon would wait close to the operating room all day.

I scrawled a quick thank-you on the back of a candy box and tucked it underneath his family picture.

It's hard to believe that more than a decade has passed. Now Sarah is fifteen years old, and I find myself recalling the rabbi who reminded me of what was at the heart of my own faith. My God does not abandon us in times of suffering. He is there because He has been through suffering Himself.

WELCOME TO HEAVEN

When I was growing up, our family life often revolved around an ice-skating rink. My sisters figure skated, and my brothers played hockey. My dad loved to watch our winter performances. He was always a presence, keeping vigil by a snowbank or behind the Plexiglas of an indoor arena. My younger brother Timmy recalls Dad's involvement in this aspect of our lives.

B ack in the winter of 1969, when I was a little boy, my dad and I made an ice-skating rink in our backyard. Set against the frozen Minnesota moonlight, I held a garden hose with mittened hands, the water freezing on its way to the ground.

My dad stood by, a six-foot-four-inch giant in a puffy down jacket.

"It's like heaven out here," he said, the smoke from his cigarette melding with the smell of hardening ice.

I looked upward, following Dad's gaze to a starlit sky. My toes were numb, curling inside my boots. My water-soaked mittens were growing a thin coat of ice.

"Heaven?" I asked. I didn't know what he meant.

The winter weeks passed while Dad and I spent many nights skating together on that homemade rink. While windchills dipped well below zero, Dad taught me how to grip a hockey stick and how to "slap shoot" a puck. Beneath a snowy firmament, Dad and I would glide around a makeshift net made of shovels and sheets, the metal blades of our skates etching curly lines on the ice.

"C'mon. Shoot it! Go for a breakaway! Don't hit the goal post!" Dad would shout, his voice echoing against the snowbanks.

He was loud. At times he was gruff. But at the end of every evening, as we gathered up equipment, Dad would quiet himself, lifting his eyes to the sky.

I knew that Dad stored the Lord in his heart, but he seldom used words to express that faith. This nightly reflection was a prayer of sorts, a way of showing me that God was important.

One night, I got tired of waiting for him to finish up his intercessions. I was cold and Mom had hot chocolate waiting for us in the kitchen.

"It'll feel like heaven when we get inside," I yelled, trying to pry him away from his winter worship.

Dad chuckled as he pulled off my stocking cap and started tickling me. We laughed all the way to the kitchen door.

Winter after winter, Dad was by my side, helping me to perfect the game. He taught me how to speed skate around orange construction cones, how to pass a puck, how to guard a goal post.

By the time I made captain of our high school hockey team, Dad was content to watch me from the sides of a new arena.

At the state tournament, as I scored the winning goal, the standing room only crowd began to clap and cheer.

But I skated past the crowded bleachers, racing my way to the goal post. There, behind a sheet of Plexiglas, Dad stood alone. I tapped the glass with my stick as Dad gave me a thumbs-up.

"Heaven!" he shouted.

As my high school years came to a close, I signed scholarship papers to attend Providence College in Rhode Island. The school was miles away from Minnesota.

It was an honor to wear the Providence uniform. I made a lot of new friends and played against the best hockey teams in the country.

Every week, I'd write Dad, sending him team programs and newspaper clippings. "I'm having a great time," I would write.

But the truth was, I'd get homesick whenever I skated in unfamiliar arenas. The space behind the goal post was always empty.

Then one Friday night in March 1985, Providence played Michigan State, a national championship game.

Before the game, as I laced up my skates, my coach told me I had a visitor waiting outside the locker room. It was my dad.

"Hey," I said, greeting him with a friendly punch in the arm.

"Not too bad a drive from Minnesota," my father quipped.

Standing in my skates, suited in shoulder pads and thick breezers, I suddenly realized I was looking down on him.

He lingered for a while, trying to put his thoughts into words.

"The good Lord is proud of you," he said, patting me on the back. It was seldom that I heard Dad talk like this.

"The good Lord is proud of you too," I replied.

The game began. As I skated past the cheering crowds, I searched for Dad behind the goalpost, but found him sitting with my mom in the bleachers, right behind the players' bench.

As our eyes met, he pointed to a banner posted high above the rink—it spanned the entire arena.

Intended to highlight the superior skill and strength of the opposing team, the banner read: "Welcome to Heaven."

I laughed to myself as the referee dropped the puck to begin the opening face-off.

The crowd roared. Minute by minute, Providence maintained a two-point lead with Michigan State. With five minutes left in the game, I scored a goal.

Looking up toward the bleachers where Dad was sitting, I

expected to see him give me a thumbs-up. Instead, I saw the team chaplain and a doctor huddled over him. There was a look of shock on my mom's face.

As an ambulance pulled up in front of an entryway that overlooked the goalpost, my coach ushered me through the jammed crowd.

Dad died fifteen minutes after I arrived at the hospital.

While the team chaplain comforted my mom, I slipped away to a large lobby window. Still clad in my skates and uniform, I watched a snow shower blanket the city. I began to recount the last few hours.

How fitting it seemed that a "Welcome to Heaven" banner had decorated the arena where Dad had passed away.

I was certain that eternity was now his inheritance, a reward for teaching me about the love of God.

He taught me about this love, not so much in well-spoken words, but in the time he spent with me. Throughout the years, Dad had stood by my side, like an ever-present heavenly Father, teaching me how to perfect the game of life.

How to share laughter.

How to offer the gift of "presence."

How to pray without uttering a sound.

As I stood there, a passage from Matthew's gospel came to mind: "The kingdom of heaven is near" (Matthew 3:2).

I understood a little better that the love between a father and a son is a bit of heaven on earth.

It has been fourteen years since that night in Michigan. Now I have three little boys of my own.

This past winter, my oldest son and I made an ice-skating rink in our backyard. As he held the garden hose with his small mittened hands, I stood by, dressed in a puffy down jacket.

Though windchills dipped well below zero, I looked upward and smiled.

"It's like heaven out here," I said softly.

THE DONUT STORY

Like my father, my younger sister, Annie, can tell a great story. At family gatherings, you can usually find her at my mom's kitchen table surrounded by young nieces and nephews. They love the way she punctuates her true-life tales with a wave of her arms by dramatizing the actions she is talking about. "The Donut Story," as Annie calls it, has become a family classic.

That Thursday morning the City Center was bustling. People packed the escalators and offices were filling with chattering workers. Annie rushed into a small bakery.

A successful sales rep, Annie was young and pretty and fiercely independent. Dressed in an expensive tweed suit and polished leather pumps, she was scheduled to give a morning presentation at her company; she had decided to buy donuts for the meeting.

As Annie signed an invoice to pay for the pastries, a heavy-set baker plopped an oversized box in front of her.

"You want some help carrying that?" the man asked. The white bakery box was almost a yard long.

"I'll be fine," Annie assured him. Gripping the center of the box, Annie steadied herself as the ends of the container began to droop.

"You're gonna need some help," the baker warned.

Annie rolled her eyes. *As if I can't carry a box of donuts…*

Carefully carrying the box—step, balance, step, balance—
Annie left the bakery holding her head as high as she could,
considering the task she had undertaken.

From a nearby bench, a middle-aged woman looked up
from her newspaper and saw Annie's slow, step-balancing
progress. Herself neatly groomed in a white pantsuit and a gold
barrette, the woman cringed as Annie approached a moving
escalator.

"You need help, honey," the woman in white said to Annie.
It was clear that the box of donuts was beginning to buckle.

"I'm okay, really I am," Annie told her.

But as Annie stepped onto the escalator, the heel of her
pump got stuck in the metal ridges of the moving stairs.

Putting down her paper, the woman rushed to Annie's aid,
jumping onto the stairs that were carrying Annie upward.

While Annie tried to pry her shoe away from the metal
stairs, the other woman tried to gain control of the collapsing
donut box.

"Whoa…" Annie said just as the lid of the box swung open
and a shower of cream puffs and bear claws began raining over
the City Center.

The two women watched as the box tumbled downward.
They gasped as glazed donuts rolled past office doors and
muffins ricocheted off the windows of quaint shops. Annie
closed her eyes as a chocolate éclair hit the head of a well-
suited businessman.

When at last Annie and the middle-aged woman stepped
off the escalator, they found their clothes covered with chocolate frosting and sprinkles.

They began to chuckle. Annie was wearing only one shoe
and the older woman's hair was completely undone—a flying
donut had unsnapped her barrette.

Then Annie laughed outright, realizing that she had
brought this small disaster upon herself. It could have all been

avoided if she had been willing to accept help.

In spite of the embarrassment she had gotten off pretty lightly though—she'd had a good laugh and made a new friend.

God had made the best of a sticky situation.

May I Have This Dance?

Preparing for Christmas sometimes can distract us from the spiritual joy that God wants to give us. I learned this last December. "Joy to the world, the Lord has come."

I ordered a bag of popcorn at the snack bar while my girls scurried through the department store searching for Christmas gifts. I yawned as the clerk handed me my snack; I could barely keep my eyes open.

We had just moved into a new home. In between unpacking boxes, I had baked cookies and wrapped presents and written cards of greeting.

So far the holidays had left me feeling depleted of energy. I hadn't even had time for prayer or quiet reflection. I wanted to feel close to God, especially in this season, but I was just too tired.

As I settled into a booth, I noticed an old, kind-faced man standing near the store entryway—he was ringing a Salvation Army bell. Though his face was wrinkled, his eyes bore the energetic twinkle of youth.

Wearing bib overalls and an ear-muffed hat, the man's skin was much darker than the lighter-faced customers who crowded the suburban store.

I watched as he danced around his red coin kettle, bobbing and turning to the rhythm of his own footsteps. Ringing his bell in carefully timed beats, he waved and smiled to those who passed him by.

"Joy to the world…whoa…the Lord…mmm…the Lord has come."

Soon a woman made her way past the singing man. She was wearing a Christmas tree sweater trimmed with ribbons and baubles. She dodged her way past the man; her brow was furrowed and she carried several shopping bags.

"No joy for the Lord?" the Salvation Army worker called out to her.

The woman sighed and rolled her eyes. She hurried to her car.

I watched as people hussled past the man, most of them ignored his presence. Everyone seemed to be preoccupied with balancing the bags and boxes that contained their purchases.

A businessman with a cell phone walked past the dancing bell ringer.

"Let every heart…mmm…prepare him room…" the dark-skinned man sang.

The businessman kept walking as the beeping noise from the cash registers forced him to shout his conversation into the phone. He reminded me of all the obligations I had for the season. I was trying to find a way to converse with God, but so far I hadn't gotten a good connection.

As countless shoppers made a point to walk a wide perimeter around the coin collector, an older woman drew near.

Though her back was hunched and her gait was slow, she smiled as she clicked open a purse decorated with beads. She dropped four quarters into the slotted red pail.

The man took off his ear-muffed hat and bowed to her.

"May I have this dance?" he asked.

The woman began to giggle and blush. As she straightened up, it almost seemed as if her wrinkles were beginning to fade.

The two of them began to shuffle around the store entry-way, the man in overalls gently guiding the frail woman in graceful glides and turns.

"Joy to the world…the Savior reigns…" their voices rang out in happy refrain.

As I watched, I found myself wanting to join their department store waltz. Theirs was a dance of Christmas joy, a dance unencumbered by stress or preoccupation, a dance of praise, a dance that proclaimed anew the tender message of old: "Joy to the world...the Lord has come!"

Later that night, as my family slept upstairs, I curled up on the couch in our family room.

Turning on my favorite holiday CD, I drank a cup of tea in front of our brightly lit tree. Soon a guitar version of "Joy to the World" filled the room.

I imagined God bowing before me. I could almost hear Him say: "May I have this dance?"

THE DIVINE TOUCH

It was a cold November night when our first baby was born and diagnosed with Down's syndrome. For a while, that winter was a season chilled with the despair of dashed dreams. It was also a season when the warmth of God touched my life in a most unusual way.

That winter, now fifteen years ago, it got so cold that ice formed inside the kitchen windowpanes. Gasoline froze in the tank of my husband's car. Bare, brittle limbs snapped in the breeze, and newscasters warned of wind-chill dangers and frostbite. Despite the bitter weather, I walked alone each morning through our new neighborhood, dressed in layers of down and wool.

I walked and I walked. Maybe defying the elements made me feel I had some control over my life. That year I had lost two loved ones to death, and our first baby was born with Down's syndrome. As much as I loved our child, I still felt stunned. God seemed concealed, hidden somewhere in this cold winter of death and disappointment. So I trudged in solitude, day after freezing day. Only in front of a stranger's blue-shuttered brick house did I become gradually aware of a presence, a kind of peace. Although my breath froze in the air, a spiritual warmth filled me. Here, for a brief moment each morning, I felt something promising, hopeful, reassuring. I didn't know why.

Spring finally did come, and children once again pedaled

bicycles on the sidewalk, men swung golf clubs on the green fairways, and I exchanged my down and wool layers for jerseys and faded blue jeans.

One morning I took my newborn, Sarah, with me on my walk. In the bright sunlight in front of the brick house, I saw a mother playing with her young twin daughters.

I watched as she gently guided the girls' hands over rough bark and offered them lilac blooms to smell. Just when I realized the children were blind, the mother greeted me with a wave.

"May they touch your baby?" she asked. While the girls softly stroked Sarah's face, brushed her fine chestnut hair, and held her tiny pink hands, their mother spoke about what it had been like when her children were born and what unexpected blessings she had found in those early years. "In adversity we must be alert," she said, "for God will find a way, somehow, to touch us."

I wondered if I should tell her about my walks. Finally I said, "Last winter when I passed by your home each morning, I felt strangely reassured and comforted. Warmed."

My new friend smiled. "You must be the person I felt compelled to pray for this winter," she said. "I thought someone in this neighborhood was going through a difficult time. Now I know it was you."

MORE IMPORTANT THINGS

My husband grew up with Paul Molitor, the professional baseball player. Every now and then, Paul calls or stops by for a visit. Recently Paul shared a touching story with our family.

A parade of convertibles lumbered through downtown Toronto while half a million people crowded the streets. Two days earlier, the Blue Jays had won the World Series. Now my teammates and I were the focus of a nationwide celebration.

I waved to the throngs from the back of a white convertible, my wife, Linda, and my nine-year-old daughter at my side. Fans were perched on window ledges and lampposts, blowing horns and throwing confetti and waving the Canadian flag.

I felt the inexplicable thrill of a once in a lifetime moment. This was the highlight of my professional career. It was unforgettable.

"Look, Blaire," I pointed out a businessman waving a sign that read: "MVP—Molitor for Prime Minister."

"Daddy," she said with a giggle, "that would be a great job for you."

Amid the roar and revelry of celebration, my thoughts began to drift. "Someone else should be here," I thought. Soon the face of a little girl appeared in my memory, the face of Lauren Ball.

I first met Lauren in July of 1991 when I was living with

my family in Milwaukee. At that time, I was playing third base and was designated hitter for the Brewers; I also served on the board of Midwest Athletes against Childhood Cancer (MACC). That year MACC sponsored a fashion show, and I was asked to model an outfit with Lauren who would soon be celebrating her ninth birthday.

Just before the show, the two of us stood together behind stage, waiting for our turn to walk down the runway.

Though Lauren was wearing a wig and had lost several pounds from two recent surgeries, she stood straight and proud, holding a magic wand that matched her flowered jump-suit.

I, on the other hand, kept readjusting my tie and tapping my foot. I wanted to start a conversation, but I didn't know what to say. Lauren sensed my uneasiness. As our names were announced to the audience, she linked her arm firmly in mine, gliding me down the runway like she was leading me in a dance.

"Look, Paul. There's my mom and dad…and my baby brother Luke…" she confidently pointed out to me. I turned to find her parents, Scott and Heidi, snapping pictures. The audience couldn't stop clapping and cheering—Lauren had won their hearts.

"You were the star of the show," I told her behind stage.

"No…you were." She smiled warmly.

A few months later, Make-A-Wish of Wisconsin contacted me. Lauren had a wish: She wanted to meet me at spring training coming up soon in Arizona. I agreed to donate some batting lessons to help finance the trip.

On a Saturday afternoon, I met Lauren and her family at a local batting cage. After a few hours of giving free baseball tips to youngsters from the Milwaukee community, Lauren presented me with a gold Make-A-Wish star. It was Lauren's way of saying thank-you for donating the lessons.

It was really nothing, I told her. Secretly, I was embarrassed at all the attention. My small contribution of time could never compare with the courage of a little girl facing cancer.

"No...it was really something," Lauren insisted. "Now I get to see you in Arizona."

When Lauren arrived in Arizona, Make-A-Wish made sure that her family's motel room was decorated in Brewers colors. In between shopping and sightseeing, Lauren would come and watch my games. From the baseball field, I could see her in the stands, this smiling little girl in a Brewers jersey, holding a baseball glove.

I couldn't help but feel a little awkward. Lauren was waving and cheering for me. I thought it should be the other way around.

Before one of the Arizona games, I met Lauren outside the locker room.

"How's my buddy?" I asked as I handed her some Brewers souvenirs.

She just wrapped her arms around me and wouldn't let go. "Have a great game, Paul," she said.

In early summer, Make-A-Wish made arrangements for Lauren to throw out the first pitch at a Brewers game. Just before the game, I interviewed her on the evening news.

"What kind of pitch are you going to throw?" I asked. As the camera focused in on Lauren, she sat quietly, as if in deep thought.

"Curve or fastball?" I interrupted. I thought she might need my help.

Lauren just smiled, a twinkle in her eye: "I'm gonna throw it straight, I guess."

And she did.

Throughout that summer and into the fall, Lauren became my favorite fan.

In between seeing each other at Brewers games, we would

meet at a batting cage or go out for ice cream or just call each other on the phone.

"How are you feeling, buddy?" I would always ask.

Whether Lauren was feeling strong or going through a grueling treatment, she would always answer that question in the same way: "Just fine."

She was more interested in talking about my life: How were the Brewers doing? Are you ready for a winning streak? Are you still eating Rice Krispie bars?

She was a good friend.

When the snow fell and the Christmas season arrived, I visited Lauren at her home. Though her parents reported that Lauren was still doing well, I noticed she seemed tired. I had just signed as a free agent with the Toronto Blue Jays. I didn't know how Lauren would feel about the news.

"Paul...it's okay...it's a good decision," she said.

I couldn't help but chuckle. She sounded just like a psychiatrist trying to affirm my choice.

"Look on the bright side," she continued. "Now I'll have two favorite teams."

As we drank hot cider in front of her decorated tree, Lauren and I exchanged gifts. I gave her a chocolate baseball and a crocheted angel that Linda had picked out.

Lauren closed her eyes and hugged the angel tightly. "Thanks," she whispered.

She placed a small package in my lap. "For you," she said.

Inside were two turtledove charms, small enough to attach to a chain. Enclosed was a card that read: "Keep one and give the other to a very special person. Turtledoves are a symbol of friendship and love."

Lauren took one of the doves and placed it in my hand.

"We'll be friends forever," she said softly.

Later that night, I attached the chain to my workout bag.

As the winter weeks passed, my family and I made

preparations to move to Toronto. Meanwhile Lauren's condition began to worsen. One cold night in late January, I got a phone call from Lauren's mom. She reported that doctors had discovered a large tumor behind Lauren's left eye.

"We're going to try an experimental treatment at Duke in North Carolina," she went on.

"Can I talk to Lauren?" I asked. Heidi handed her daughter the phone.

"Hey, buddy, I'll come and visit you tomorrow," I told her.

The next day Linda and I arrived at the hospital. Though Lauren was becoming weak from medical procedures, she had no interest in sharing the details of her progressing disease. "Do you think you'll be happy in Toronto?" Lauren asked. I felt like I was talking to a peer.

"Linda and I found a house. When you get better, you can come and visit us." A week later, Lauren began the experimental treatments at Duke. After a series of tests and surgery, doctors concluded that their efforts had failed.

Lauren returned home and continued to receive intensive treatment at Children's Hospital in Milwaukee. I, on the other hand, traveled to Florida for spring training with the Blue Jays. While I was there, I called Children's Hospital almost every day.

Lauren rarely mentioned her treatment or surgery or the pain she was in. Instead, she reminisced about our friendship: the fun she had had at the fashion show, the pitch she had thrown so "straight," the Christmas presents we had exchanged.

In late spring, after the Blue Jays season had started, the team traveled to Cleveland for a game. That afternoon before heading to the ballpark, I called Lauren's hospital room to see how she was doing.

"Lauren doesn't have much time left," Heidi said.

After receiving special permission from the Blue Jays, I booked the first flight into Milwaukee.

That same night, as I stood beside Lauren's bedside, I hardly recognized her. She was hooked up to IVs and beeping monitors; her face was pale and swollen.

Nonetheless, her eyes were bright and her smile, like always, was radiant and very much alive. Her baseball glove was lying on her pillow.

After hugging Heidi and Scott, I knelt down next to her bed.

"How's my buddy?" I asked.

"Just fine..." she whispered. On her bedside table was the turtledove charm. "I waited for you all day," Lauren said, smiling. In the moments that followed we laughed, we cried, we remembered the special times we had spent together.

"Shall we say bedtime prayers?" Heidi asked.

Scott and I nodded.

As I folded my hands, I listened as Lauren and her family recited a prayer:

Dear Father in heaven,
Look down from above.
Bless Mom and Dad, Lauren, Luke...and Paul...
And all those whom I love.
May angels guard over my slumber, and when
Morning is breaking,
Awake me...
Amen

Lauren died a few weeks later on May 23, 1993.

Five months after her death, the Toronto Blue Jays went on to win the World Series, and I was riding in a convertible in a downtown parade of ticker tape and decorated cars, waving to an applauding crowd.

As our convertible steered its way into the Sky Dome stadium, fifty thousand fans began to chant, jabbing their index fingers in the air in accompaniment: "We're number one! We're number one!" In the midst of it all, I found myself thanking God that He had brought this little girl into my life.

She would have loved this, I thought.

Though her time on earth was short, she had taught me some of the most important lessons I have ever learned: Always smile, set others at ease, cheer for those you love, be like Christ.

I recalled a verse from the Bible: "Whoever wants to become great among you must be your servant, and whoever wants to be first must be slave of all" (Mark 10:43–44).

I realized that Lauren had accomplished this call of Christ; she had been a good friend and a good servant. This was her life achievement, an even greater accomplishment than winning the World Series.

Later that night, after all the partying was over, I carried my little girl into her room and tucked her into bed. I wanted to give her the "there are more important things in life" talk; I couldn't wait to share all that Lauren had taught me. But Blaire just nodded off, tired from all the day's events.

As I pulled a blanket over her, I gazed at my little girl's face. I was grateful for her presence; just watching her breathe made me thankful for her life. She was a precious gift entrusted to me by the grace of a loving God.

I could trust that someday soon Blaire would meet a "Lauren" too. God would see to that.

And so, I knelt beside my daughter's bed and tried to remember the words of Lauren's prayer:

Dear Father in heaven,
Look down from above,
Bless Linda and Blaire…and Lauren…
And all those whom I love…

TEACUPS OF LOVE

I always smile when I see a decorative teacup in a gift shop.
These days, teacups are very popular, but Mema collected
them long before the current trendiness.

When I was a little girl, every Sunday morning was like a holiday. After church, my family, all eleven of us, would gather in my grandmother's kitchen. Wrapped in the scents of warm cinnamon rolls and the sounds of small talk and percolating coffee, "Mema" would make her rounds, hugging us tightly, one by one, as if she hadn't seen us in years. Soon aunts and uncles and countless cousins would arrive. Everyone loved Mema.

One Sunday morning, when I was nine years old, Mema's kitchen got a little crowded. I slipped away from the noisy congestion of family into Mema's dining room. It was a much quieter place where warm sunlight streamed through paned picture windows and guilded rose prints adorned the walls.

Next to a drop leaf table was a china hutch filled with polished teacups. During the hard years of the Great Depression, Mema had received each cup as a gift, a secondhand gift from a moneyless friend or relative.

"They're cups of love…priceless," Mema used to say.

That morning I found myself admiring the porcelain patterns of the keepsake cups: every petaled rose, each silver-edged heart, every etching of emerald ivy.

"Some day I'll collect teacups," I told myself as I pressed my hands against the glass doors of the hutch.

Mema peeked in on me from the kitchen. Drawing near, she saw me studying her collection.

"Which one do you like best?" she asked, smile wrinkles framing her cocoa brown eyes.

"That one!" I pointed to a sunlit cup; it was lavender, trimmed with strands of gold leaves.

Sixteen years later, on my wedding day, I opened a small package that Mema had wrapped with foil white paper. Underneath a lacy bow, she had tucked in a card. "Your favorite," it read. As I held the gift in my hand, I knew it would be the first teacup in my collection.

The early years of my marriage passed quickly. My husband and I didn't have much money, but I could always find a few dollars for the teacup hidden by the chipped punchbowls and worn Tupperware of a garage sale.

By the time my second child arrived, I had scraped the peeling paint from an old glass-doored cabinet, refinishing it with a coat of maple stain. Since I now had a "hutch" of my own, I gradually filled each shelf with secondhand teacups. I placed Mema's wedding gift cup in the middle of the collection—it would always remain my favorite.

But while I was busy adding cups to my hutch, Mema was giving hers away. She was growing older and weaker, a cancer invading her bones; nonetheless, she made sure that her keepsake cups found a home.

Like me, each of my sisters received one on her wedding day. So did the brides of my brothers and cousins. Every grandchild got a "cup of love."

A few weeks after my third child was born, Mema's health began to worsen.

I visited Mema one last time while my husband watched the kids.

Before I reached the bedroom where she lay, I passed

through her dining room. Stopping for a moment, I pressed my hands against the glass doors of the hutch and peered inside. All of the cups were gone; only lines of sunlight filled the shelves.

Moments later, I sat at her bedside.

"Mema," I whispered. "Your teacups...were they hard to give away?"

Mema took my hand. Though her breathing was labored, her eyes were warm and brown and bright.

"They were cups of love...and love is meant to be shared," she replied. As Mema drifted off to sleep, I closed my eyes with a clear and lovely image.

Mema's life was like a beautifully patterned teacup, brimming with a lifetime of unforgettable tenderness, given to our family as a gift.

She was like a "keepsake" passed down to us from God, ours to cherish deeply, ours to admire forever in the "hutches" of our hearts.

A few years have passed since Mema died. I miss her but my three young daughters remind me that she is never really far away.

Recently, on a sunlit Sunday morning, I watched them study my shelved array of keepsake cups.

Together, they memorized the porcelain patterns; every petaled rose, each silver-edged heart, every etching of emerald ivy.

"Which one do you like best?" I asked Rachael, my youngest.

She pointed to a lavender cup trimmed with strands of golden leaves. "That one!"

A DAY FOR HEROES

My uncle Bud holds a special place in my heart; his picture hangs prominently on a wall in our living room. Though he died in 1944, I know that he was a great hero. My grandmother told me so twenty-five years ago on a sunny Memorial Day morning, a morning that began with a parade.

I leaned against an oak at the side of the road, wishing I were invisible, keeping my distance from my parents on their lawn chairs and my younger siblings scampering about. I hoped none of my friends saw me there. God forbid they caught me waving one of the small American flags Mom bought at Ben Franklin for a dime. At sixteen, I was too old and definitely too cool for our small town's Memorial Day parade. *I ought to be at the lake,* I brooded. But no, the all-day festivities were mandatory in my family.

A high school band marched by, the girl in sequins missing her baton as it tumbled from the sky. Firemen blasted sirens in their polished red trucks. The uniforms on the troop of World War II veterans looked too snug on more than one of them.

"Here comes Mema," my father shouted.

Five black convertibles rolled down the boulevard. The mayor was in the first, handing out programs. I didn't need to look at one. I knew my uncle Bud's name was printed there, as it had been every year since he was killed in Italy. *Our family's war hero.* And I knew that perched on the backseat of one of the cars, waving and smiling, was Mema, my grandmother. She had a corsage on her lapel and a sign in gold embossed letters on the car door: "Gold Star Mother."

I hid behind the tree so I wouldn't have to meet her gaze. It wasn't because I didn't love her or appreciate her. She'd taught me how to sew, to call a strike in baseball. She made great cinnamon rolls, which we always ate after the parade. What embarrassed me was all the attention she got for a son who had died *twenty years earlier.* With four other children and a dozen grandchildren around, I couldn't figure out why this was such a big deal every year.

I peeked out from behind the oak just in time to see Mema wave and blow my family a kiss as the motorcade moved on. The purple ribbon on her hat fluttered in the breeze.

The rest of our Memorial Day ritual was equally scripted. No use trying to get out of it. I followed my family back to Mema's house, where there was the usual baseball game in the backyard and the same old reminiscing about Uncle Bud in the kitchen. Helping myself to a cinnamon roll, I retreated to the living room and plopped down on an armchair.

There I found myself staring at the army photo of Bud on the bookcase. The uncle I'd never known. I must have looked at him a thousand times—so proud in his crested cap and knotted tie. His uniform was decorated with military emblems that I could never decode. Funny, he was starting to look younger to me as I got older. *Who were you, Uncle Bud?* I nearly asked aloud.

I picked up the photo and turned it over. Yellowing tape held a prayer card that read: "Lloyd 'Bud' Heitzman, 1925–1944. A Great Hero." Nineteen years old when he died, not much older than I was. But a great hero? How could you be a hero at nineteen?

The floorboards creaked behind me. I turned to see Mema coming in from the kitchen, wiping her hands on her apron. I almost hid the photo because I didn't want to listen to the same stories I'd heard year after year: *Your uncle Bud had this little rat terrier named Jiggs. Good old Jiggs. How he loved that mutt! He wouldn't go anywhere without Jiggs. He used to put him in the rumbleseat of his Chevy coupe and drive all over town. Remember how hard Bud worked after we lost the farm? At haying season he worked all day, sunrise to sunset, baling for other farmers. Then he brought me all his wages. He'd say, "Mama, someday I'm going to buy you a brand-new farm. I promise." There wasn't a better boy in the world!*

Sometimes I wondered about that boy dying alone in a muddy ditch in a foreign country he'd only read about. I thought of the scared kid who jumped out of a foxhole in front of an advancing enemy, only to be downed by a sniper. I couldn't reconcile the image of the boy and his dog with that of the stalwart soldier.

Mema stood beside me for a while, looking at the photo. From outside came the sharp snap of an American flag flapping in the breeze and the voices of my cousins cheering my brother at bat. "Mema," I asked, "what's a hero?"

Without a word she turned and walked down the hall to the back bedroom. I followed.

She opened a bureau drawer and took out a small metal box, then sank down onto the bed.

"These are Bud's things," she said. "They sent them to us after he died." She opened the lid and handed me a telegram dated October 13, 1944. "The Secretary of State regrets to inform you that your son, Lloyd Heitzman, was killed in Italy." *Your son!* I imagined Mema reading that sentence for the first time. I didn't know what I would have done if I'd gotten a telegram like that.

"Here's Bud's wallet," she continued. Even after all those years, it was caked with dried mud. Inside was Bud's driver's license with the date of his sixteenth birthday. I compared it with the driver's license I had just received. A photo of Bud holding a little spotted dog fell out of the wallet. Jiggs. Bud looked so pleased with his mutt.

There were other photos in the wallet: a laughing Bud standing arm in arm with two buddies, photos of my mom and aunt and uncle, another of Mema waving. *This was the home Uncle Bud took with him,* I thought. I could see him in a foxhole, taking out these snapshots to remind himself of how much he was loved and missed.

"Who's this?" I asked, pointing to a shot of a pretty, dark-haired girl.

"Marie. Bud dated her in high school. He wanted to marry her when he came home." *A girlfriend? Marriage?* How heartbreaking to have a life, plans and hopes for the future, so brutally snuffed out.

Sitting on the bed, Mema and I sifted through the treasures in the box: A gold watch that had never been wound again. A sympathy letter from President Roosevelt and one from Bud's commander. A medal shaped like a heart, trimmed with a purple ribbon. And at the very bottom, the deed to Mema's house.

"Why's this here?" I asked.

"Because Bud bought this house for me." She explained how after his death, the U.S. government gave her ten thousand dollars, and with it she built the house she was still living in.

"He kept his promise all right," Mema said in a quiet voice I'd never heard before.

For a long while the two of us sat there on the bed. Then we put the wallet, the medal, the letters, the watch, the photos, and the deed back into the metal box. I finally understood why it was so important for Mema—and me—to remember Uncle Bud on this day. If he'd lived longer he might have built that house for Mema or married his high-school girlfriend. There might have been children and grandchildren to remember him by. As it was, there was only that box, the name in the program, and the reminiscing around the kitchen table.

"I guess he was a hero because he gave everything for what he believed," I said carefully.

"Yes, child," Mema replied, wiping a tear with the back of her hand. "Don't ever forget that."

I haven't. Even today with Mema gone, my husband and I take our lawn chairs to the tree-shaded boulevard on Memorial Day and give our three daughters small American flags that I buy for a quarter at Ben Franklin. I want them to remember that life isn't just about getting what you want. Sometimes it involves giving up the things you love for what you love even more. That a man lay down his life for his friends was how Christ put it. That many men and women did the same for their country—that's what I think when I see the parade pass by now. And if I close my eyes and imagine, I can still see Mema in her regal purple hat, honoring her son, a true American hero.

THAT'S THE WAY I FEEL ABOUT YOU

When our daughter Sarah was five years old, our family faced unexpected financial hardship: Bills relating to her disability kept on mounting. Though it was a time of great uncertainty, God found a way to let us know that He loves us.

One hot July morning, I awoke to the clicks of a broken fan blowing humid air across my face. The well-used fan had seen better days. It had only one setting, and its blades were worn and bent. It needed repair. So, I thought, did my life.

Earlier that year, Sarah had undergone heart surgery. That was all behind us, but now we faced mounting medical bills that insurance wouldn't cover. On top of that, my husband's job would be eliminated in just weeks, and losing our home seemed inevitable.

As I closed my eyes to try to put together a morning prayer, I felt a small hand nudge my arm. "Mommy," Sarah said, "I g-g-got r-r-ready for v-v-vacation B-B-Bible school all by myself!"

Next to the bed stood five-year-old Sarah, her eyes twinkling through thick, pink-framed glasses. Beaming, she turned both palms up and exclaimed, "Ta-dah!"

Her red-checked, seersucker shorts were on backward, with the drawstring stuck in the side waistband. A J. C. Penney price tag hung from a new, green polka-dot top. It was inside out. She had chosen one red and one green winter sock to go with the outfit. Her tennis shoes were on the wrong feet, and she wore a baseball cap with the visor and emblem turned backward.

"I-I-I packed a b-b-backpack, t-t-too!" she stuttered while unzipping her bag so I could see what was inside. Curious, I peered in at the treasures she had so carefully packed: five Lego blocks, an unopened box of paper clips, a fork, a naked Cabbage Patch doll, three jigsaw puzzle pieces, and a crib sheet from the linen closet.

Gently lifting her chin until our eyes met, I said very slowly, "You look beautiful!"

"Thank y-y-you." Sarah smiled as she began to twirl around like a ballerina.

Just then the living room clock chimed eight, which meant I had forty-five minutes to get Sarah, a toddler, and a baby out the door. As I hurried to feed the kids while rocking a crying infant, the morning minutes dissolved into urgent seconds. I knew I was not going to have time to change Sarah's outfit.

Buckling each child into a car seat, I tried to reason with Sarah. "Honey, I don't think you'll be needing your backpack for vacation Bible school. Why don't you let me keep it in the car for you."

"No-o-o-o. I n-n-need it!"

I finally surrendered, telling myself her self-esteem was more important than what people might think of her knapsack full of useless stuff.

When we got to church, I attempted to redo Sarah's outfit with one hand while I held my baby in the other. But Sarah pulled away, reminding me of my early morning words, "No-o-o-o…I l-l-look b-b-beautiful!"

Overhearing our conversation, a young teacher joined us. "You *do* look beautiful!" the woman told Sarah. Then she took Sarah's hand and said to me, "You can pick up Sarah at 11:30. We'll take good care of her." As I watched them walk away, I knew Sarah was in good hands.

While Sarah was in school, I took the other two children and ran errands. As I dropped late payments into the mailbox and shopped with coupons at the grocery store, my thoughts raced with anxiety and disjointed prayer. What did the future hold? How would we provide for our three small children? Would we lose our home? Does God really care about us?

I got back to the church a few minutes early. A door to the sun-filled chapel had been propped open, and I could see the children seated inside in a semicircle listening to a Bible story.

Sarah, sitting with her back to me, was still clutching the canvas straps that secured her backpack. Her baseball cap, shorts, and shirt were still on backwards and inside out.

As I watched her, one simple thought came to mind: "I sure do love her."

As I stood there, I heard that still, comforting voice that I have come to understand is God's—"That's the way I feel about *you.*"

I closed my eyes and imagined my Creator looking at me from a distance: my life so much like Sarah's outfit—backward, unmatched, mixed up.

"Why are you holding that useless 'backpack' full of anxiety, doubt, and fear?" I could imagine God saying to me. "Let Me carry it."

Though this tender message of love was spoken in the quietness of my heart, I think it was a message that most of us long to hear. When our lives seem backward, inside out, and out of control God calls us to trust that what we need will be provided.

It is in these vulnerable times of weakness that we need to

give our fear-filled backpack to the One who says, "You are precious and honored in my sight, and because I love you" (Isaiah 43:4).

That night as I once more turned on our crippled fan, I felt a renewed sense of hope. That day Sarah reminded me that God's presence remains even when life needs repair. She had been a messenger of God's love. What a privilege to parent such a child.

STEVIE'S WISH

When we bought our last home, I got to know my realtor,
Karla. During a long drive to a house showing, Karla
talked about her volunteer work with an organization that
grants wishes to terminally ill children. "That must be
rewarding. Tell me about it," I said as we drove down the
freeway.

K arla, a busy real estate agent, had a beautiful home in
the suburbs and three healthy children. She was grateful for all her blessings and had always given generous
financial gifts to local charities. Still, she felt that something
was missing.

One morning as she drove to meet a client, she listened to a
local radio host talk about Make-A-Wish, a program that grants
wishes to children with terminal and life-threatening illnesses.
Volunteers were needed to launch the now nationally recognized foundation.

She had just finished a term with the chamber of com-
merce. She didn't want to run again. She felt she wanted to give
of her time in a different way. The program caught her attention, but she felt a little hesitant to call the broadcasted number.

"How can I make a difference in the life of a dying child,"
she wondered.

Nonetheless she found herself picking up the phone to volunteer. Soon she was giving time to the organization, one afternoon a week.

One day, as Karla sifted through the Make-A-Wish mail, she found a letter from the parents of a Down's syndrome boy.
It read:

Dear Make-A-Wish:

My son, Stevie, has leukemia; the doctors tell us he doesn't have much time. He's been wishing for a dressy suit to wear to church. Stevie would need it to be custom-made as he is short and a little bit pudgy.

My son is hoping to have his suit by Easter Sunday. With the holiday just a few weeks away, we are unable to pay for his wish. Any help would be appreciated.

Sincerely,
The O'Mallys

One week later, on a morning when the last of the winter snow was beginning to melt, Karla knocked on the door of a small inner-city home.

Mr. O'Mally answered the door.

"I'm here to take Stevie to his fitting," Karla said.

"Please come in," he said. Karla saw Mrs. O'Mally and Stevie getting up from the couch in the living room.

Standing about four feet three inches, Stevie was round and portly. Though his breathing was labored, his almond-shaped eyes were bright and full of mischief.

While Karla and the parents exchanged small talk, Stevie turned on an old polka tape.

As the blasted volume of an accordion vibrated against the walls, Karla reached out for Stevie's hands.

"Let's dance," she said.

"No, no," he said, his face turning a little red. "I just had a baby," he told Karla, smiling and patting his stomach.

Mrs. O'Mally rolled her eyes. "Oh, Stevie," she scolded. She turned to Karla and said, "His sister just had a baby."

"A joke…a joke…" He laughed aloud.

"Come on, Stevie, give it a try." Karla tried one more time.

The two of them linked hands and hopped and jerked around the living room, their unmastered steps awkward and clumsy.

After a few minutes of dancing, Stevie turned to his mother.

"You dance?" he asked.

"I don't know how to polka," his mother said.

"That's A-okay," he said, taking her hands and gently swinging her in a circle.

But soon it became clear that Stevie's disease was taking its toll on his energy level.

He flopped in an armchair, trying to catch his breath. A few minutes later he said, "Time to go buy my Easter suit."

After Stevie had taken some medication, Karla and Stevie drove to an exclusive men's store.

Standing in front of a full-length mirror, Stevie held his head high, even though he was wearing worn elasticized jeans and a flannel shirt with a button missing.

While the salesman slid the tape measure around Stevie's rounded waistline, the Down's syndrome boy stood statue-still, his arms outstretched like the wings of a plane.

"Yellow is my favorite color," Stevie told Karla as the clerk wrote down measurements. "Can I have a yellow tie?" he added.

"I think we can arrange that," Karla said as she pulled a golden silk tie from a rack on the counter.

While Karla signed an invoice to pay for the suit, a crisp white shirt, and a pair of patent leather shoes, Stevie ran his hands over the smooth fabric of the tie. He grinned.

"Now I'll look just like the ushers," he told Karla.

Easter Sunday came.

Early that morning, Karla arrived at the O'Mallys' church, hoping to catch a glimpse of Stevie in his Sunday finery. She sat in a back pew.

Just before the choir began to sing the opening hymn, "Christ the Lord Has Risen Today," Stevie appeared. He walked down the sunlit center aisle, his mother and father a few steps behind.

With stately posture, he proudly nodded to the ushers and the smiling congregation, stopping to adjust his yellow tie with every third step.

Karla was struck by the change in Stevie's appearance. From a four-foot-three-inch boy, Stevie had been transformed into a well-dressed man. It was almost like he was six feet tall.

She wanted to clap in applause.

Four days later, Karla received word that Stevie had died.

After the funeral luncheon, Karla went for a long walk around a nearby lake. Stevie had died peacefully in his home; he was buried in his custom-made suit. Surrounded by spring-time flowers, newly bloomed, she found herself offering prayers of gratitude.

God had shown her that a small gift, even a little bit of time, can make a big difference in someone's life. In giving only a few hours to the O'Mally family, she had gained something too. Spending her time with Stevie had brought her unforeseen joy.

With a smile on her face, she imagined him walking into the kingdom of heaven, tall and proud, wearing the suit he had wished for in life.

She thought of him adjusting his Easter-yellow tie, transformed in the light of eternity, now healed and whole.

She could almost see him nodding to a smiling God, his almond-shaped eyes full of everlasting sparkle.

Karla wanted to prolong the heavenly image, but as she walked past a flower-framed path, her cell phone rang.

It was Make-A-Wish.

"Can you spare a couple of hours?" the caller asked.
Karla paused to pick a yellow tulip.
"I'll be right over."

A GOODWILL CHRISTMAS

Most of us have at least one Christmas memory that we will never forget. Mine is easy to recall, although it took place several years back when the kids were small.

We were having financial struggles; nonetheless, our family received a gift that cannot be bought with coin or check or charge card.

T he clock chimed eight o'clock; the house was quiet and still. My three children, all very young at the time, were fast asleep. I sat on the living room couch in front of a blinking Christmas tree mending a rip in my bathrobe. I had worn this old orange terry cloth robe for over a decade, and it was frayed at the hem and missing two buttons.

"I need mending too," I told God.

It had been a hard year for our family. Among other things, my husband had lost his job, and although he was working odd jobs at night, there was little money in the budget for Christmas presents and certainly not money for a new robe.

In spite of our limited funds, I had gone to a department store earlier that day searching for inexpensive gifts for the kids. With only twenty dollars and a little loose change in my purse, I had quickly steered my shopping cart toward the back of the store where the bargains tended to be. And sure enough there was a table piled high with cheaply priced toys, crayons, marbles, and small books. After selecting a few things for each of the kids, I made my way to the checkout line.

While waiting to pay for my purchases, I had watched the woman in front of me unpack a cart filled with expensive porcelain dolls, electronic trucks and trains, and two children's computers. The woman had unblinkingly written out a check for over $350. I was not without a little envy. Then I happened to glance toward the sleepware department where a mannequin sported a red velour bathrobe with shiny pearl buttons. And for a moment I imagined myself in the plush, regal-looking robe.

As I pulled a needle and thread through the tear in the sleeve of my ratty robe, I couldn't help sighing and wishing we had more money.

The phone rang, startling me out of my thoughts.

"N-N-Nancy...this is G-Gretchen."

She didn't really need to announce herself; I recognized her voice immediately. Gretchen was limited in many ways, but she did manage to work a minimum-wage job and lived in a subsidized home with her sister Kay, also disabled.

"C-C-Can y-your f-f-family come over t-t-tomorrow night?"

I glanced at the calendar hanging by the phone. My husband was free, but it was one of the few nights he'd had off in weeks. I wasn't entirely sure I wanted to give up the limited time we had for our family to spend together.

Just then I overheard Kay's voice in the background. "Can they come? Can they bring the kids?"

After I heard her excitement, I couldn't find it in me to decline the invitation.

"We'll be there at six," I promised, and then I jotted down directions to their house.

The following evening, my husband and I bundled our children into snowsuits and fur-lined boots. Light snow fell as we traveled down the freeway, the kids singing "Jingle Bells" from the back seat.

My husband reached out to take my hand, a sweet thing

that told me he was up for this little adventure. But I scarcely noticed. I was too preoccupied with worries about finances. I just looked out the car window and watched the gentle snowfall.

Soon enough, we turned down a street lined with tall pine trees. Driving past cheery, snow-covered homes decorated with colored lights and glittery door wreaths, we stopped in front of a small paint-worn house with warped shutters.

The kids wiggled out of their car seats, leaping through the snow and blazing a path to the front door.

A living room light illuminated the two sisters waiting at the front picture window.

Gretchen opened the door and immediately wrapped her arms around us. "You're here!"

"The kids came too," Kay said with excitement, her eyes twinkling.

Gretchen, short and slender, wore a mismatched outfit of checkered bell-bottoms and a striped satin shirt. Kay, heavyset, wore a sleeveless Hawaiian print dress. It was clear they had dressed up for the occasion.

While Don knelt to help the kids take off their boots, I looked around the kitchen. Orange flowered wallpaper rippled at the seams, the floor was buckling, and six empty boxes of Rice-A-Roni were stacked on the table like a centerpiece, the rice now bubbling in a kettle on the stove.

"W-W-Would anyone l-l-like a s-s-soda?" Gretchen asked.

"Sure," said my husband.

"Can we have some, Mom?" the kids chimed in as everyone followed Gretchen into the living room.

There, instead of furniture, were several cartons of Diet Pepsi, stacked like bleachers. The kids began to count the boxes of soda. "There's a hundred in all," they exclaimed.

"S-S-Soda's cheaper w-w-when you buy it in b-b-bulk," Gretchen said.

I could not suppress the giggles as I climbed the stairway of soda crates to drink a Diet Pepsi next to Don, who was also chuckling.

Meanwhile, the kids ascended to the top of the bleachers, jumping off with happy squeals and rolling across the orange shag carpet.

"This is fun!" they said.

After a paper plate dinner of piled-high rice and pink mints, Gretchen and Kay brought out a huge plastic bag.

"It's t-t-time f-for p-p-presents," Gretchen announced.

Inside the bag were several gifts wrapped in newspaper and duct tape.

"W-w-we b-b-bought t-them at the G-G-Goodwill," Gretchen said. Her smile was truly as big as I've ever seen it.

We watched the kids open present after present: a broken train, a chipped tea set, a faded Santa Bear.

"Look what I got, Mommy. See, Daddy?" they shouted with excitement, unaware that the toys had once been used and discarded.

When Don opened his gifts, an outdated World Series T-shirt and a hat from Mel's Bait Shop, Gretchen and Kay began to cheer in jest: "Try them on! Try them on!"

I burst out laughing. It felt so good. It seemed as if I hadn't laughed in months.

"You look great," I told Don in between giggles.

"W-W-We have one more p-p-present," Gretchen said as Kay slipped into a back bedroom. She reappeared with a package wrapped in exquisite gold paper and a red velvet bow.

"F-F-For y-you," Gretchen said, and she placed the gift in my lap.

Wondering what was inside, Don and the kids drew close, watching me closely, as curious as I was about what might be in such a beautifully wrapped box.

Beneath layers of neatly creased tissue was a brand new

bathrobe: pink velour with heart-shaped buttons. A price tag still hung from the robe's sleeves; it had come from an exclusive store.

"I w-w-won it at m-my C-C-Christmas p-party at work," Gretchen said. "I thought it m-m-might look p-p-pretty on y-you."

I immediately slipped the robe on over my clothes. I twirled and bowed and everyone oohed and ahhed with delight.

My eyes met Don's and I smiled.

"There's a m-mirror in the h-hallway," Gretchen said.

As I took a look at my reflection, I noticed a small photograph tucked into the mirror's frame. It was a picture I had given Gretchen months earlier, a snapshot of Don and me and the kids.

I took the photo in my hands.

Just a day earlier I had wished for more money, as if money could buy the priceless gift that Gretchen and Kay had just given to us—the gift of selfless love.

In sharing what little they had, their humble home, their lovingly prepared rice, their duct-taped presents, Gretchen and Kay had given us the priceless treasure of laughter and joy even in the midst of hardship. Something we had needed far more than fancy things.

They had shown us how much more important people are than things, things that will eventually chip and break and rip. That love is the only gift that becomes more valuable when it is recycled.

Even a brand new bathrobe could not compare with the love that these two sisters had so carefully packaged.

Later that night as we drove home and the windshield wipers whooshed away the falling snow, Don reached out to hold my hand; I held his tightly.

We had been richly blessed. We had each other. We had the kids. We had received the gift of selfless love in an unexpected place.

It was enough.

DROP EARRINGS

My friend Laurie shared a story from her childhood with me a few years back. Her memory tells of the power that truth has to transform one's life. "This story will bring hope to many...I'll write it someday," I promised her then. Laurie, I always keep my word!

We had come to the park that day to celebrate my thirty-fifth birthday. We were two enduring friends, both mothers with three children apiece. From a picnic table we watched as our kids laughed and leapt their way through a playground fragranced with scarlet apple trees and lavender lilacs.

It was a good day for a picnic. Dressed in shorts, denim jackets, and sunglasses, we unpacked a basket bulging with bologna sandwiches, Doritos, and Oreo cookies. We toasted friendship with clear bottles of mineral water.

It was then I noticed Laurie's new drop earrings—tiny interlocking loops of silver laced with stones of indigo blue. For the thirteen years I'd known Laurie, she had always loved drop earrings.

Over the years I'd seen her wear pair after dangling pair—threaded crystals cast in blue, shiny silver loops, strands of colored gemstones, sapphire hoops, beaded pearls in pastel pink, diamonds set in golden links.

"There's a reason why I like drop earrings," Laurie said.

———

When Laurie was in the sixth grade, her desk was the last in a row of seven near a bank of brick-framed windows. She remembered with amazing detail the way her classroom looked one spring day—the yellow May Day baskets suspended on clotheslines above her desk, the caged hamsters that rustled through shredded newspapers, the window shelves where orange marigolds curled over cutoff milk cartons, the cursive writing charts above the blackboard. That classroom felt safe to Laurie, a sharp contrast to a home riddled with problems.

"Mrs. Lake made the classroom feel so safe," Laurie said. She recalled the way her teacher looked on that long-ago morning; how her auburn hair flipped onto her shoulders like Jackie Kennedy's, how her kind, hazel green eyes were full of light and sparkle.

But it was her teacher's drop earrings that Laurie remembered most, golden teardrop strands laced with ivory pearls. "Even from my back row seat," Laurie recalled, "I could see her earrings gleaming in the sunlight from the windows." They provided a beacon of hope in a dark, depressing life.

That year her father's alcoholism had escalated. Many late nights she had fallen asleep to the sounds of his disabling disease: whiskey being poured into shot glasses, can openers piercing metal beer tops, ice cubes clicking in glass after glass, the loud slurred voices of her father and his friends in the kitchen, her mother's sobs, slamming doors, pictures rattling on the wall.

The previous Christmas she had saved baby-sitting money to buy her dad a shoeshine kit, complete with varnished footrest, a buffer brush, and a copper can of Cordovan shoe polish. She had wrapped the gift with red and green Santa Claus paper and trimmed it with a gold ribbon curled into a bow.

On Christmas Eve she had watched in stunned silence as he

threw it across the living room, breaking it into three pieces.

Laurie took off her sunglasses and began to rub her eyes. I handed her a napkin. I could see that the pain of that Christmas memory still lingered.

Laurie returned to the story of that day in the classroom. "That spring day had been set aside for end-of-the-year conferences. Mrs. Lake stood in front of the class reminding us that both parents and students would participate in these important progress reports." On the blackboard an alphabetical schedule assigned a twenty-minute slot for each family's conference.

Laurie was puzzled that Mrs. Lake had placed her name at the end of this list, even though her last name began with a B. It didn't matter much—her parents would not be coming. She knew this despite the three reminder letters she'd seen at home and the phone calls her teacher had made.

All day long she listened as the volunteer room mother called out her classmates' names. Laurie watched each child being escorted past her desk to a doorway five feet away, a doorway where parents greeted their sons and daughters with proud smiles and pats on the back and sometimes even hugs. The door would close.

Though she tried to distract herself with assigned projects, she couldn't help but hear the muffled voices just beyond the door as interested parents asked questions, children giggled nervously, and Mrs. Lake offered affirmations and solutions.

She imagined how it might feel to have her parents greet her at that door.

At last, after everyone else's name had been called, Mrs. Lake quietly opened the door and motioned for Laurie to join her in the hallway.

In silence she slipped out without any of her classmates noticing. There were three folding chairs set up in the hallway across from a desk covered with student files and projects.

Curiously she watched as Mrs. Lake began to fold up two of the folding chairs. "These won't be necessary," she said. Laurie sat down in the remaining chair. Her teacher looked through Laurie's files and smiled.

Laurie folded her hands and looked down at the linoleum floor; she was embarrassed her parents had not come.

Moving her chair next to the downcast girl, Mrs. Lake lifted Laurie's chin so that she could make eye contact with her. "First of all," she began, "I want you to know how much I love you."

Laurie lifted her eyes. In Mrs. Lake's face, she saw things she'd rarely seen—compassion, empathy, tenderness.

"Second," she continued, "you need to know that it is not your fault that your parents are not here today."

Again Laurie looked into Mrs. Lake's face. No one had ever talked to her like this. No one had ever given her a way to see herself as anything but worthless. No one.

"Third," she went on, "you deserve a conference whether your parents are here or not—you deserve to hear how well you are doing and how wonderful I think you are."

In the following minutes, Mrs. Lake held a conference with Laurie—just Laurie. She showed Laurie her grades and Iowa test scores and academic charts that placed her in the upper national percentile. She scanned papers and projects that Laurie had completed, always praising her efforts, always affirming her strengths.

She had even saved a stack of watercolor paintings Laurie had done.

"You would be a great interior designer," she said. Laurie didn't know exactly when, but at some point in that conference she remembered hearing the voice of hope in her heart, somewhere in that inner place where truth takes hold and transformation starts.

And as tears welled up in her sixth-grade eyes, Mrs. Lake's

face became misty and hazy, all except for the auburn curls and ivory pearls of her drop earrings.

Laurie realized, for the first time in her life, that she was lovable.

We sat together in the comforting silence that follows a story worth remembering. In those quiet moments, I thought of all the times Laurie had worn the drop earrings of truth for me.

For years I had been haunted by insecurity, always feeling my life held little worth or value.

But Laurie had met me in a symbolic hallway of empathy. There she had shown me that self-worth is a gift from God that everyone deserves, a precious jewel, bestowed at birth to be worn with pride for a lifetime.

She had helped me to see that even adulthood was not too late to don the diamonds of newfound self-esteem, to finally define myself as valuable.

Just then the kids ran to the table, dramatizing famine by flopping onto the grass and picnic benches.

For the rest of the afternoon, we found ourselves immersed in the interruptions of parenthood. We cut bologna into small pieces, wiped up spilled milk, praised off-balance somersaults and glided down slides much too small for us.

But in the midst of it all, Laurie handed me a small box, a birthday gift wrapped in red floral paper trimmed with a gold bow.

I opened the box. Inside was a pair of drop earrings.

My Commander Was God

I've known my father-in-law for nineteen years. In that time, I've rarely heard him talk about his experience as a POW in World War II. When I asked him if I could write a story about his wartime captivity, he sent me a twenty-five page reflection about it.

Morning, fellas," our commander said. Wearing an Eisenhower jacket, he stepped onto a stage, its only prop a covered screen. All the airmen stood and came to attention. "At ease," he said as he unveiled a map of Europe.

It was early February 1945. America was at war with Germany. At twenty years of age, I was attending a morning briefing at an air force base in England.

"Our target for the day…" the commander announced as he explained that our force would be attacking a synthetic fuel plant located deep in East Germany.

Sighs of hesitation rippled through the soldiers. Plants of this type were supplying Germany with 70 percent of their fuel; they were fiercely defended with antiaircraft artillery and fighter planes. Missions like this were more dangerous than others we flew.

There was a collective uneasiness, and I felt a sense of foreboding. Though I was part of a force that included 1300 bombers and 800 escorting fighter planes, I knew I wasn't invincible to the enemy.

As I rushed off to get ready for the flight, I passed a small room occupied by the group's chaplain. Along with several other men, I stopped for a short preflight prayer service. As the chaplain prayed a blessing I thought about my mortality. Would I come back from this mission alive?

"Let us join together in saying the Lord's Prayer," the chaplain said.

I hurried through the prayer; I had recited it a hundred times before.

Later, I donned my helmet and tucked a pocket New Testament and a wristwatch into my heated flight jacket. After eating a breakfast of toast and eggs, I boarded our aircraft manned with a crew of nine members. As we climbed in altitude, we joined a formation of countless bombers—a line of planes that probably stretched for over two hundred miles.

I was proud to be a part of this magnificent display of military power.

As we flew over the English Channel, we began to climb to 25,000 feet. Four hours later we neared the synthetic fuel plant, as hundreds of flak guns began to fire from below. The once blue sky now became clouded with bursting shells. In the dimmed light, we began to release our bombs.

Shortly after completing our bombing run, we heard a loud banging noise. Suddenly the plane began to falter as two of our inboard engines received direct hits.

"Shut down the engine and feather the props," the pilot ordered through the intercom.

Now at half power, our plane was damaged. Unable to maintain altitude and speed, we were forced to leave the protective covering of our formation.

We flew on alone for about twenty minutes. Not one of my fellow crewmen spoke; it was an eerie silence. Now we were vulnerable to enemy aircraft searching for our planes.

"Abandon the aircraft," the pilot shouted, as over a dozen

enemy fighters began to attack us.

I jumped from the plane in a whirling free fall. At five thousand feet, I pulled the ripcord of my parachute. As it deployed, a white canopy blossomed out to cushion my downward plunge.

When I landed in a plowed field, I rolled up my parachute and ran into a nearby grove of trees. Discarding the flying equipment and hiding it in some brush, I realized that I was alone.

I didn't think to pray for God's help. I was too preoccupied trying to figure out how I could avoid capture. Relying on my inner resources I reasoned: "Maybe I can escape the enemy under the cover of darkness."

As I continued to strategize, a civilian search party surrounded me. They were local farmers and townspeople. They waved pitchforks and one of the group members held a rusty gun. I raised my arms to show them I was unarmed.

After the search party ushered me to a nearby farmhouse, they confiscated my belongings: my Bible, watch, and helmet, placing them in a box. It was only then I began to realize the graveness of my situation.

"I am a prisoner of war," I told myself.

The reality of those words brought on a wave of anxiety. I was now at the mercy of a foreign enemy. I had no family, no comrades, no military support.

"Our Father who art in heaven…" I prayed.

About a half hour later, two armed men in German uniforms escorted me to the nearby town of Eisenach. There I was taken into a government building where I was interrogated by a military officer and his female secretary.

After writing down my name, rank, and serial number, they pressed me for more information.

"As a POW, I am not obligated to give you any more information," I told them.

I wasn't sure how they would respond to my refusal. I had heard of American prisoners who had been tortured for not submitting additional details.

As the German officer looked over my belongings, he took the New Testament in his hands.

"What's this?" he asked in German as he waved the book at his secretary.

"A Bible," she interpreted in a soft voice.

The officer paged through my Bible, as the secretary motioned me to a large window that overlooked the small town. In the distance, I could see a majestic looking castle nestled in the hills.

"Martin Luther translated the Bible there," she said. She went on to explain that he was kept there for a full year, in the protective custody of his friends. Her eyes were full of kindness.

I looked at the stately mansion and thought about Luther. So many years earlier he had taken the time to withdraw from the world, to listen to the voice of God.

Maybe it's my turn to listen, I thought.

In that moment, even though I was in a land torn by war and suffering, I felt a hint of God's presence. Somehow I knew He was near.

The next morning, German guards marched me and several other members of my crew to the rail yards at the edge of town. Along the way we were met by an angry group of civilians. The night before, Allied forces had bombed a nearby village. We saw that in the center of town, the hostile crowd had hung several British airmen by the cords of their parachutes.

The people began shouting and swearing; they picked up stones to throw at us. Raising their hands in anger, several people reached out to pull us into the uncontrolled mob. The guards hurried us to a nearby train where we were locked in boxcars.

The train carried us to an undisclosed location. I lay down on some straw. I was cold and hungry and scared. It was hard to rest.

Up until now I had only known war from the window of an airplane, now I saw it firsthand: the hatred, torture, death, and suffering. I wanted it all to be over; I wanted my freedom; I wanted to go home....

The next morning we arrived in Oberusel, a town seven and a half miles from Frankfurt. We were taken to the Intelligence Evaluation Center and placed in solitary confinement.

A German guard pushed me into a six-by-ten-foot cell, and a heavy steel door slammed shut behind me.

Many days and nights passed while I remained locked in my cell. The absence of human conversation and even minimal comforts was a different kind of torture.

Stripped of all my personal belongings, I slept on a scratchy mattress. I never took a shower and food was sparse.

I battled loneliness. I often asked myself: "Why am I alive? Why had other men died and not me? Did God have a purpose for me in solitary confinement?"

It was hard to pray.

Sometimes I regretted that I had not memorized more passages from Scripture. Now I had time, lots of time, to meditate on His Word.

One night I found myself gripped with despair. In the darkness of my cell, a passage from the Lord's prayer surfaced in my memory.

Thy will be done on earth as it is in heaven.

An unexplained calm came over me. "God is the commander of my life," I whispered in the dim. God was my only protection; He was my fortress, my comfort, my hope.

As I got down on my knees, I knew I needed to surrender my will to Him. I needed to give Him all my unanswered questions. I needed to trust that He would sustain me through all that lay ahead. I needed to claim the power of His presence.

"Thy will be done in me," I prayed.

In the weeks that followed, I continued to fight off bouts of anxiety, but God always seemed to provide the emotional and spiritual strength I needed.

In times when anxiety overwhelmed me, I often reflected on passages from the Lord's Prayer. When I was hungry, I would ask for the "daily bread" of God's ever-present grace.

When I was angry at my captors or when I struggled to understand my role in the war, the words of Jesus would come to mind. "Forgive us our trespasses as we forgive those who trespass against us." Day after day, night after night, I was learning how to listen to God.

On April 29, 1945, my time in the POW camp finally came to an end.

Leaving behind my captivity, I returned home and married Pat, the love of my life. In time, we went on to have five children and God supplied us with much more than "daily bread."

I was blessed with a good-paying job, a nice home, and plenty of friends. The years were marked with the noise and bustle and laughter of a large family.

Now that I'm seventy-five and the kids are grown, the house gets pretty quiet. My wife passed away just a few years back.

Sometimes I get lonely, but in those times when I'm by myself with no one to talk to, I remember that God stands guard over my life, just as He did when I was in solitary confinement.

These days I spend more time with the men who fought with me in World War II. There is a veteran's hospital near my home where men continue to suffer from the effects of wartime service, but I have been spared much of this.

Maybe it's because I look back on my time in solitary confinement as a gift, albeit a strange gift, from God.

It was in my time of solitude that I met my "Commander in Chief." I discovered a God who can sustain a soul without the comfort of food or conversation or even a Bible to read.

This commander deserves my utmost respect, for He preserved me with only His presence and a simple prayer that has become the cornerstone of my faith.

Our Father who art in heaven,
Hallowed by Thy name.
Thy kingdom come.
Thy will be done, on earth as it is in heaven.
Give us this day our daily bread.
And forgive us our debts, as we also have forgiven our debtors.
And do not lead us into temptation, but deliver us from evil.
For thine is the kingdom, and the power, and the glory, forever.
Amen.

A SUNFLOWER
FOR JANUARY

They say that when people die, their life flashes before them. When I'm on my deathbed I'm sure I won't recall the houses I lived in or the cars I've driven or the balance in my bank account. What I hope I will remember are the simple moments I have shared with loved ones.

Flakes of whirling snow whooshed over the windshield of our van. It was an early Saturday morning in January, dark and cold with a windchill of twenty-two below zero.

"I wish it were spring," my twelve-year-old daughter T. T. said as I steered our car into the YMCA parking lot.

Grabbing our workout bags from the trunk, we trudged through drifts to the exercise room, our mittened hands clasped tightly.

While T. T. began to jog on a treadmill, I started my Stairmaster routine on a machine right next to hers. In between huffs and puffs, we continued to lament about winter in Minnesota.

"I can't remember what the sun feels like," T. T. said as she stepped up her jog. "Winter is such a hassle."

"And remember when the van died we had to wait three hours for help, and the new car battery cost us a hundred and fifty dollars," I added as I wiped my brow.

On a wall next to us there was a TV monitor. "Another winter storm is headed our way," the newscaster announced.

"It's hard to feel joy in January," I told my daughter as I began lifting an arm weight.

Even though we complained, I was glad to have T. T.'s company. She had been busy all week with homework and play practice. Lately, spending time together had become a challenge. Now, I looked forward to our Saturday morning workouts.

As I took a sip from my water bottle, I gazed through the glass of a large picture window that framed the exercise room. Outside, an orange sunrise lit the bare limbs of skinny trees that shivered in the wind. I closed my eyes to remember a day from the previous summer.

It was eighty-five degrees and sunny; our family was vacationing at a lakeside cabin in northern Minnesota.

While my husband fished from the dock with my two other daughters, T. T. and I lounged together on a beachside hammock.

As she talked of preteen things, friends and magazines and pierced ears, we drank Dr. Pepper and ate Doritos.

Our hammock rocked in the lake breeze. We closed our eyes and relished the feeling of the warmth of the sun on our faces.

"Tell me again about the day I was born," T. T. asked.

I was happy she had asked. I never grow tired of telling her the story. "It was snowing…you came at midnight. It was one of the happiest moments of my life," I remembered.

For the rest of the day, T. T. and I cuddled in that hammock, playing games of Old Maid and reading tearful stories from *Chicken Soup for the Soul*.

The summer memory faded as I opened my eyes. Snow-whirled winds rattled the YMCA window.

"I wish it were July," I said to T. T. as we finished our workout.

As the two of us walked to our van, pulling scarves over our faces, we saw a shiny yellow Volkswagen parked right next to us.

Curiously we peered inside the brightly colored car.

On the dashboard, a golden sunflower curled from a small crystal vase. Next to the vase was a stuffed bunny and a small toy Volkswagen, both the same sunny shade of yellow as the car.

"Look, Mom," T. T. said as she pointed to a long silver plate attached to the glove compartment. It read: Don't postpone joy.

At first T. T. looked puzzled, but then she started to laugh. I laughed too, even though the bitter winter winds were snapping against our jackets.

"Maybe God is trying to tell us something," I said with a giggle.

I realized that joy is a gift that God gives to all his children, a gift that we can claim on any day or in any season, a gift that we should never put on hold.

Happiness need not be dependent on a warm summer breeze or a beachside hammock, but on the simple moments we are given to share with others, sacred moments that we can easily miss.

As we drove home behind a snowplow, I reached out to hold T. T.'s mittened hand.

"Mom...let's stop and buy a sunflower," she said.

We did.

GOD HAS A PLAN FOR YOUR BABY

*When I first began my teaching career, I learned that the
teacher-student role may sometimes be reversed.*

The hospital room was wrapped in early-morning darkness as bright flakes of November snow fell outside the window near my bed. My husband slept soundly on a cot next to me, but I drifted in and out of restless sleep.

I kept replaying events from the night before: labor…pain…a baby…a diagnosis.

I remembered clearly the doctor's midnight words: "I'm sorry, Mr. and Mrs. Sullivan…preliminary findings indicate that your baby has the symptoms and tendencies of Down's syndrome."

The digital clock blinked 7:02 A.M. I was worn out and tired. I wanted to sleep but unanswerable questions kept me from rest.

What did the future hold?

How would we adjust?

What would we tell our families?

Then I heard a knock at the door. I saw the silhouette of a young, pony tailed girl in a pleated skirt, her outline shadowed by the dim lights of the hospital hallway.

As she moved closer, I rubbed the tiredness from my eyes

to make out the face. It was Jessie. We smiled, simultaneously. As she sat down in a chair next to my bed, I called to mind memories from a September morning just the year before. I was newly graduated from college; it was the first day of my teaching career.

I had been assigned to Room 202, in a Catholic high school.

As the school bell sounded through the aging brick corridors, twenty-one sophomores entered my 8:00 A.M. homeroom: a fifteen-minute block of time that proceeded scheduled classes, a time reserved for announcements and bureaucratic tasks.

The students were all girls, all uniformed in the black woolen pleats and white starched collars of an eighty-year tradition. Carrying backpacks weighted with college prep books, they squeaked to their desks in polished saddle shoes.

"I'm Mrs. Sullivan," I announced as I wrote my name on the blackboard.

Jessie, along with the other girls in the class, watched closely and whispered. I too was uniformed, but I knew that my navy blue tweeds and professional pumps could not conceal my youth and inexperience.

But as the mornings passed, those homeroom whispers found a voice in the brief conversations we began to exchange.

Sometimes we talked about academic pressures. The girls were worried about getting good grades for college.

Other times the topics were more lighthearted. Especially on Monday morning when the girls bantered about the weekend: basketball games and slumber parties, dances and dresses and dates.

But somehow it always seemed that those homeroom conversations flowed into curious questions about my life.

What had my first date been like?

Was the college I attended a good one?

How did I meet my husband?

I never grew tired of their inquiries or of sharing my life with them.

They were like younger sisters eager for advice and insight. And though my college professors had warned against becoming too "friendly" with the students, I was honored to offer what little I had learned about life.

The year passed quickly. Then one spring morning in May, I came to homeroom clutching a picture of the ultrasound I had gotten just a day earlier.

Revealing that I was pregnant, the girls cheered and teased about maternity clothes and support hose. They agreed unanimously that surely the baby would be a girl.

Then as I uncreased the black-and-white ultrasound picture that outlined the baby's heart and head and hands, they gathered around my desk—all except Jessie. She stood back from the group, her pony tailed blond hair framing a somber half-smile and blue eyes that hinted at sadness.

As homeroom ended at the sound of the bell, the girls rushed off to their first-hour classes, but Jessie lingered behind.

"Mrs. Sullivan...can I talk to you?" she asked, her voice low, almost a whisper.

"Sure," I said as I glanced at my teaching schedule; I was free until nine o'clock. We sat down in side by side desks.

"I'm pregnant too," she said, her eyes now welling up with tears.

"I'm almost four months along...I don't know what to do. My mom is divorced. She's worked hard to afford my tuition. How am I going to tell her? What will she say? What will she do if I can't stay in school?"

For a moment, Jessie just covered her face with her hands.

"It's okay, Jessie...tell me more," I said.

When she gained her composure, she talked about the baby's father, a football player from the boy's school across the street.

"He's been nominated for an athletic scholarship. We both know we're too young to get married, too young to take care of a baby. I'm so scared, Mrs. Sullivan."

As I listened, I wasn't sure if she would receive the words I felt compelled to say, but I offered them nonetheless.

"Jessie," I began. "God has a plan for your baby. Don't ever forget that." As the last days of school approached, Jessie and I met often to talk.

During that time, Jessie told her mom about the pregnancy and found unforeseen compassion and comfort along with a loving coach to support her through birthing classes.

I, in turn, met with the principal to strategize how we as a school might help Jessie and her family during the remaining months of her pregnancy.

Much to Jessie's surprise, the school invited her to return to classes in the fall, even though her due date was mid-October, just six weeks before mine.

All through the summer months, I thought of Jessie as I gathered gifts at baby showers and when I shopped for car seats and crib sheets and bumper pads.

Every time I felt the motions and movements of my baby, I couldn't help but visualize her meeting with social workers and signing adoption policy papers and paging through biographies of perspective parents.

Her plans and preparations for birth were so much different than mine....

When the autumn days of early September arrived, Jessie greeted me in the doorway of Room 202. Wearing a plaid maternity top, blue jeans, and tennis shoes, she waved her class schedule at me. "I'm in your homeroom again, Mrs. Sullivan!"

We tried to hug each other but found it impossible. Our stomachs were the same size: enormous. We laughed.

Four weeks later, Jessie delivered a healthy baby girl. After a few days of recovery, she was back in homeroom neatly uniformed. She showed me pictures of the baby she had given away, the daughter she had cradled in the hospital for a few short hours.

"I told her that I loved her, Mrs. Sullivan...."

Now Jessie was visiting after the birth of my baby nearly a month later, to welcome my Down's syndrome daughter.

She had come in the early morning hours, before school, to offer me the words I had once offered her.

"God has a plan for your child, Mrs. Sullivan; don't ever forget that."

I looked at her and smiled.

For so many months I had felt compelled to teach her to trust in God's plan. How well she had learned that lesson. She knew it by heart. Now trust was the tender lesson she could teach me.

Several years have passed since that snowy November day. Just a few weeks back as I waited in my car at a corner stoplight, Jessie pulled up right next to me in a station wagon.

I waved. She honked.

There was a baby sleeping in a car seat. When the light changed, she drove away, but my Down's syndrome daughter and her two younger sisters called out from the backseat, "Who was that, Mommy?"

I smiled.

"That was a teacher I once knew," I said. "One of the best."

STRANGE WAYS

When I was a kid, my father gave new meaning to the words: "God works in strange ways."

Rachael ran on ahead of us making her way toward the back of the department store to the bike section. It was her sixth birthday, and my husband and I had promised her a new bike.

The three of us surveyed a row of new bikes: testing kickstands and turning tires and comparing prices. Rachael smiled. She was wearing bib overalls and a baseball cap.

"There's my dream come true!" she said as she pointed to a pink-fendered bike with a yellow seat and fringe-trimmed handlebars.

An older woman in a "Best Grandma" sweatshirt looked on as she passed us by with her shopping cart. "Is this your first bike?" she asked. Her face was beaming.

Rachael nodded, her grin betraying a loose front tooth.

"She just learned how to ride," my husband told her as he helped Rachael onto the seat.

The woman moved on and a young couple strolled by hand in hand. "Look…she's getting her first bike," the twenty-something woman told her boyfriend as Rachael gave the bike a "test ride" through the sporting goods department.

My husband and I followed behind at a slow jog as Rachael steered past a young father and his son. They were trying out fishing poles.

"Be sure to get her a helmet," the father suggested.

All the way to the checkout lanes, shoppers paused to watch Rachael peddling her new bike. It was almost like she was in a parade: the store aisle was lined with smiling people who nodded and tipped their hats—some of them even clapped.

"Most people remember their first bike," I told Rachael as we stood in line to pay for her birthday present.

"Do you remember yours, Mommy?" my little girl asked.

I laughed. My thoughts wandered back to a hot July evening in the mid-'70s. Back then, I was a preteen, the third oldest of eight brothers and sisters.

As I ate dinner with my family at a long wraparound bar in the kitchen, my little brother Johnny waved an advertisement he had clipped from the newspaper.

"Ten speeds are 20 percent off at Montgomery Ward," he announced. My mom handed Dad the clipping as he took a loud swishy gulp of coffee and studied the ad.

My father was a big man with a gruff demeanor. He wore golf shirts and black-framed glasses like the '50s rock star, Buddy Holly. There was mystery in him. He only spoke when he needed to, and we never really knew what he was thinking.

He was a good provider, making a decent salary at an insurance company, just enough to make ends meet.

None of us had bikes. They were too expensive. Still, we couldn't help dreaming about the trendy ten speeds that were so popular at the time.

"Can't afford bikes," Dad said as he puffed on his Camel cigarette.

In between bites of mashed potatoes, my brothers and sisters and I continued to share visions of handlebar brakes, metallic finished fenders, and shiny gears that shifted with a click.

Later that evening, just before we dozed off to sleep, my father made his usual rounds past our rooms.

"Keep the faith," he called out from the dimly lit hallway where a cross hung on the wall. It was Dad's way of reminding us to remember God's loving presence in our lives.

As the night hours passed, the air grew hot and muggy, and it was hard to sleep. At about 1:30 in the morning, I looked out my bedroom window and saw Dad sitting on the picnic table in our backyard. Beneath the starlit sky, the crickets chirped as Dad bowed his head and folded his hands. I wondered what he was praying for.

Early the next morning, I heard my father start up our Chevy station wagon. Around noon, he returned home, the car trunk filled with an odd assortment of junk: rusty flat pieces of metal, stuffed bits of leather, twisted rubber tubing.

While my brothers and sisters and I did our usual Saturday chore of digging weeds from the front yard, we saw Dad drive into the garage and close the door behind him.

"What's he thinking?" Johnny asked me as he pulled on the roots of a dandelion.

"Maybe he went to the junkyard again," I answered as I clipped a row of crabgrass.

Every now and then, Dad went to the city dump to search for treasures: a piece of old furniture, a usable shovel, a repairable cabinet for the garage.

Over the next two weeks we heard him working behind the closed garage doors. We heard pounding and metal scraping and whooshing noises. He worked in secret day after day, posting an OFF LIMITS sign on the garage siding.

Finally, one Sunday morning before church, he called us together in the driveway. We crowded around him in a quiet, curious hush. Ever so slowly, he opened the garage door, like the unveiling of a stage curtain.

We peered inside.

There, lined up in a homemade bike rack were nine recon-
ditioned bikes, each coated in a different shade of semigloss.
The fenders were wide and mismatched, the tires were fat,
overpumped with air and looked like they were ready to burst.
Each recycled seat was rippled with duct tape, and spray-
painted baskets were attached to nine chunky handlebars.

With a proud sweeping motion of his arm, Dad presented
the bikes to us, his head held high.

Johnny turned to me. "The seats are stuffed." He giggled.

"A basket," my older sisters gasped. They were teenagers. At
that time a bike basket was the unconcealable mark of a neighborhood nerd.

"No way," my younger sisters whispered. Their bikes and
mine had orange handlebar horns, the rubber squeezable kind.

As my dad led my littlest siblings to three small bikes
trimmed with hot pink training wheels, my mom stood by, trying not to laugh.

"Try 'em out!" Dad said. From our driveway, he watched in
pride as the nine of us rode down our street in one self-
propelled drove, our pudgy tires clacking and rattling.

When we had pedaled around the block, far from Dad's
sight, a metal screw sprang from the wheel of Johnny's bike.

"Whoa!" Johnny whooped as his front tire detached and
began rolling solo down a steep hill.

The rest of us hit our brakes and watched as the out of control wheel rolled through a busy intersection, cars honking. We
cringed as it narrowly missed Mrs. Bottomley, a neighbor trimming her rosebushes.

When at last the spinning tire came to rest in a hedge, my
brothers and sisters and I turned to find Johnny still clutching
the handlebars of his now wheelless bike.

We all started laughing at the same time. "What was Dad
thinking?" we all wondered as we doubled over, snorting and
slapping our knees.

What was he thinking? I asked anew as my husband and I loaded our daughter's bike into the trunk of our van.

Though it had been several years since Dad's death, I think I now know the answer.

All parents want to grant their children's dreams, I thought. That's why Dad had gone to such great lengths to fashion such an unforgettable collection of mismatched cycles. Without the resources of money, he had found a way, admittedly a strange way, to make our dreams come true.

Even though the pudgy-pedaled bikes bore little resemblance to the ten speeds we had hoped for, the junkyard bikes would forever represent something more valuable. Dad loved us.

"God works in strange ways too," I told myself. I thought about times in my life when God had made known a plan that seemed extremely odd, times when I had laughed at His leading, times when I had asked my heavenly Father, "What are you thinking?"

Only in time had I come to understand that God's handiwork is always a perfect expression of His everlasting love.

That night as I tucked Rachael into bed, she couldn't stop talking about her new bike. I kissed her good night. I was glad that my husband and I had the resources to provide for her.

Still I wondered, what would she remember years from now about the day she received her first bike?

That we loved her?

I hope so.

A MOTHER BLESSED

"Who has blessed us in the heavenly realms with every spiri-tual blessing in Christ" (Ephesians 1:3). *Sometimes heaven's blessings are hidden in everyday situations.*

That winter morning as I walked into the grocery store, I felt exhausted. I had been up most of the night; all three of my kids had chicken pox.

Standing in the checkout line, my basket filled with color-ing books and Sprite and Tylenol, I found myself fighting back tears.

"I want someone to take care of me," I thought.

As the clerk rang up my purchases, an elderly man in a blue store uniform stood attentive at the end of the counter.

"Do you want paper or plastic, honey?" he asked. Though his back was hunched and his hands betrayed a tremor, his eyes were full of warmth and kindness.

"Paper is fine," I said.

After packing my goods in a couple of brown bags, the two of us walked to my car, his steps slow and shuffled.

"Nice day," he said. "Even in January the sun still feels warm."

I looked up. He was right. The rays of the winter sun felt mild on my face. For a moment I allowed myself to notice that the sky was a cloudless blue. I breathed in the clean, chilly air, surrendering the tension in my muscles.

"The good Lord wants us to notice things like that," he said.

I smiled as he meticulously placed my groceries in the backseat of my car, "just right."

"God bless you," he said, waving good-bye.

As I drove home, I kept repeating the old man's words, "God bless you." For the rest of the day, I found the energy I needed to care for the kids.

Whether it was taking thermometer readings or giving baths or rocking little bodies to sleep, I reminded myself that I was a "mother blessed."

That day, someone had taken care of me.

BLIZZARD BLESSING

In the last six years, my family and I have moved three times. I'm sort of a professional at this now. Not only have I learned how to expertly pack boxes at breakneck speed, negotiate the intricacies of getting the utilities changed, and manipulate monstrous rental trucks through less than ideal traffic situations, I've learned, more importantly, that the misgivings of leaving one neighborhood will always be replaced by the comfort of new found friends in the next— friends like the ones in this story.

Peering through the early morning darkness outside her kitchen window, Shannon could feel cold air seeping through the sills. Twelve inches of blowing snow swirled and drifted over sidewalks, rooftops, and front porches. It was a "whiteout," a Minnesota blizzard.

Shannon and her family had just moved into the neighborhood. She didn't know anyone yet, and she missed the familiarity of next-door friends, the streets she knew by heart, the backyard where her kids used to play. With her husband and children fast asleep, the new home was stark and quiet, with moving boxes stacked in every room. Shannon felt wrapped in loneliness.

"Take away the emptiness," she prayed.

Snowflakes whirled against the glass panes. As she looked toward the street, she saw the headlights of a small station wagon. In front of the car, a tall man in a down jacket was shoveling a pathway for the front tires.

It was clear that the road was impassable; the snow was hemming him in on every side.

"Can I help you?" she called out from the front door, the wind biting her face.

The man rested for a moment on his shovel as a young woman opened the passenger door of the car. She was pregnant, very pregnant.

"My contractions are really close together," she said. She shivered as she pulled a scarf around her face.

In an instant, Shannon was zipping up her jacket and lacing up her boots. Then she bounded through layers of snow to their car. "We tried to call 911...they can't get an ambulance through," the man said. His eyelashes were caked with snowflakes.

He explained that they had just moved in, pointing to a split-level just two houses down from hers. "We're new to the neighborhood; we don't know anyone," he said.

Shannon turned her glance to a green-shuttered house across the street. Just the morning before she had seen a woman leave for work dressed in surgical blues. "I think there's a nurse there, in that house," she said, pointing. "I'll go see."

Abandoning his snow-covered car, he guided his wife back home.

"By the way," he called out, "I'm Stan, and this is my wife Lynne."

Lynne managed to wave, smiling and wincing in pain, all at the same time.

With no time to waste, Shannon trudged to the green-shuttered home and knocked on the door.

A middle-aged woman dressed in a nursing uniform answered. She held a cell phone to her ear.

"I can't get in for my morning shift," Shannon overheard her say. She must have been talking to the hospital where she worked.

The woman clicked off the phone and greeted Shannon with a smile. "You just moved in, didn't you? I'm Joanne," the woman said.

Shaking from the cold, Shannon could barely catch her breath to introduce herself.

"Our neighbors need a nurse...they're having a baby. They are having it right now!" Shannon said. She explained that Lynne's contractions were only a few minutes apart.

"Looks like God wants me to work my morning shift after all," Joanne said as she rushed to a closet to gather some first-aid equipment, placing it in a lidded box.

Within minutes, the two of them were blazing a path to Stan and Lynne's house. Bundled in earmuffs and mittens, they linked arms for balance.

They heard a voice call out from behind them: "Wait!"

They turned to find a uniformed policeman clad in an orange snow-drenched hat. Holding a walkie-talkie, he wore a name tag that said Scott.

"I picked up a 911 call," he shouted above the gusting winds. "Someone in our neighborhood is in trouble," he added.

"We'll take you there," Shannon said.

Without hesitation, Joanne and Shannon reached out for his mittened hands, the three of them bearing each other up as they walked through hip-deep drifts to Stan's driveway. They were met by two teenage boys. They too had picked up the 911 call on a short wave radio. They were now intent on shoveling Stan and Lynne's walk.

"We live across the street...it's the least we can do," the boys replied.

Stan appeared in the entryway. Lynne was beside him. Her eyes were closed to bear the pain of a contraction.

That's when Shannon saw it...a blue light flashing in the distance. Even through the snow-veiled darkness, the light got brighter and brighter.

"It's a snowplow!" one of the teenage shovelers yelled.

Behind the plow were a caravan of police cars and an ambulance, flashing red rays of light.

Lynne looked toward the snowplow light and her face lit up.

Stan looked upward as if he were offering a prayer. "Thank you," he whispered.

Soon no less than twelve policemen were waving flashlights, escorting Lynne and Stan to the waiting paramedics.

As the ambulance edged its way out of view, Shannon huddled with Joanne and Scott and the two teenagers. Even though the cold was biting their toes, they stopped to cheer before going inside, raising their mittened hands in the air like Sylvester Stallone in the movie *Rocky*.

An hour later Shannon got a phone call. It was Stan. "We have a son," he said. Shannon could hear the pride in his voice.

"What's his name?" Shannon asked.

"Adam," Stan answered. "And he and Lynne are both fine!"

Stan explained that their baby was born just minutes after they arrived at the hospital.

"Thanks for being there. You were a ray of hope," he said.

As Shannon hung up the phone, she realized that the emptiness she had felt that morning was gone.

Even in the midst of her own loneliness, she had been able to help a neighbor in need, to be a beacon of hope in someone else's storm, to be like a snowplow light. In the darkness there glowed the warmth of newborn friendship.

That evening Shannon and her husband invited Joanne and Scott and the teenagers along with their families over for homemade pizza and hot chocolate.

With the fireplace crackling, they happily toasted the birth of Adam, their newest neighbor. During the celebration, Shannon clicked on the six o'clock news. Soon Stan and Lynne appeared on the television screen.

Still in their hospital room, they cradled a baby wrapped in blankets.

From Shannon's family room, the new friends listened as Stan recounted the blizzard birth and how the "people next door" had come to their aid.

"We have a great neighborhood," Lynne told the television audience.

A WAY OUT

This past winter as I was driving the kids to school, I found myself listening to a Christian talk show, a nationally broadcast program. The featured guests were talking about a recent church shooting at a Baptist church in Fort Worth, Texas.

I was moved as I heard one mother, Laura MacDonald, recount how she and her Down's syndrome daughter had survived the ordeal. After dropping the kids off, I immediately called the radio station and asked if I could contact her. I sent off a card, and a few days later Laura called me.

We talked on the phone for some time—as mothers of handicapped children, we bonded immediately. As she was remembering that tragic night, I asked if she would like to share her recollection in a story. "If God can use this story to help others," she responded, "who can stop Him?"

That Wednesday evening, I combed my daughter's hair in front of a gold-framed mirror in her bedroom. As I placed a pink clip on her ponytail, I gazed at her reflection in the glass.

Just an inch over four feet tall, Heather stood proudly in her pink-striped T-shirt and matching pants. Though Heather was eighteen years old, as a Down's syndrome teenager she still maintained a childlike appearance.

"We're going to listen to music tonight," I told her as we made our way to the car. She smiled.

Earlier that morning, students from all over the Fort Worth area had gathered around school flagpoles to pray for their teachers and fellow students. To celebrate this prayer event, our church, Wedgwood Baptist, had scheduled a youth rally. Part of the program would include a Christian rock concert. Since I worked at the church as a publications secretary, I had observed the planning of the concert. I knew that over 350 young people would be attending.

What I didn't know is that the night ahead would hold unspeakable terror.

As I helped Heather buckle her seatbelt, my thirteen-year-old son, Doug, jumped into the backseat. He'd been on the phone most of the afternoon.

"All of my friends are coming to the concert," he said excitedly.

As the three of us drove to church, we stopped to pick up a sandwich for Sarah, my seventeen-year-old. Sarah was part of the drama team at Wedgwood. She was already at the church practicing a skit. Her performance would take place after the concert.

Arriving at the church a few minutes early, Doug took off to join a group of his middle school friends. After dropping off Sarah's sandwich, Heather and I mingled with friends in the foyer of the church.

"Hi, Mrs. McDonald," a young girl said. Wearing bib overalls, she passed out programs and waved. It was always good to see Mary Beth. She was a smiling blond teenager who was always involved with youth activities.

"I like your pink clip," she told my daughter as she gave her a hug. Heather smiled at her and returned the hug.

As the band began to warm up, Heather and I made our way into the church and took a place in the back row. That night my husband, Bruce, was teaching a mission class. I told him to meet us in the back of the church if he got out early.

The church became crowded with young people, along with several adults. The band adjusted microphones on a platform in front of the pie-shaped sanctuary.

After a few words of introduction, the drums began to beat, electric guitars began to vibrate, and the band members broke into songs of contemporary worship.

The young people clapped and cheered. Some of the adults jokingly put their hands over their ears and rolled their eyes. It was clear their gestures were all in fun.

An unmistakable joy rippled through the church. From wall to wall, young voices of praise were loud and strong and full of irrepressible energy. Seeing so many young people gathered to worship God was quite a sight to behold.

Right next to me, a young woman named Kim was singing so loud that I began to giggle. Though she was just twenty-three and a seminary student, the two of us had sung together on Sunday mornings in the church choir. I had never seen anyone praising God in such an uninhibited fashion.

As our eyes met, she giggled too. "I can't help it," she laughed as she joined in the next verse.

As I put my arm around Heather, she began rocking to the beat of the band. I thanked God for the gift of life, Heather's life, and all the lives around me.

It was then I heard a series of popping sounds, loud, cracking, banging sounds coming from the foyer.

With the band playing so loudly, most of those gathered in the church were unaware of the unsettling noise. In the corner of my eye, I saw Mary Beth running toward Heather and me from a nearby doorway.

Still holding a stack of programs, she screamed: "There's a gunman in the foyer!"

She rushed to my seat. Her eyes were full of panic.

"Hit the floor!" I yelled.

As Mary Beth and I dropped to the ground, Heather shook

her head defiantly. "Noooo..." she called out. Unaware of the danger we were in, she insisted on remaining seated.

When Mary Beth saw me struggling to get Heather down, she put her left arm around my daughter's neck.

"C'mon, Heather," Mary Beth whispered as she tried to pull my daughter to the floor. With Heather still defiant, the two of us huddled over her as the gunman entered the sanctuary and began firing. In between rounds of bullets, he shouted obscenities.

I knew I needed to remain calm, for Heather and for Mary Beth, but deep inside I felt fearful. Where were my other children? Was my husband safe? Would we die at the hands of this evil man?

Amid my private panic, Mary Beth began to pray aloud. She was scared. She didn't realize that the volume of her voice would attract the gunman.

"Shhhh..." I told her as a bullet hit the row ahead of us.

The gunman paced behind our row, shooting and yelling: "You Baptists think you know everything..." I focused my thoughts on protecting Heather and Mary Beth.

Three memorized words from Scripture came to mind: "God is faithful." Those words took me back eighteen years.

I smelled the smoldering of spent cartridges. I closed my eyes and remembered one of the happiest days of my life.

I held my newborn daughter in my arms. My husband stood by my hospital bed. A year earlier I had lost a child through miscarriage, so we were especially joyful with the birth of our first child.

"She's a beautiful baby," I told my husband Bruce.

Early the next morning, a pediatrician stopped by my hospital room. As I brushed the sleep from my eyes, he told me he suspected that Heather had Down's syndrome.

"In the past, children like this were usually placed in an institution, but I don't recommend it."

The doctor was a Christian. I think he sensed that I would never place my baby in a state hospital. I had already lost one baby; I wasn't going to lose another.

"Take her home...we'll do a blood test to confirm the diagnosis," he added.

In the weeks following her birth, I spent a lot of time in the library reading up on her disability.

As I scanned book after book, I realized that Heather would have many limitations, academically and socially. Her health would be an ongoing concern as well.

Though I knew parenting Heather would be full of challenges, I was offended when authors would use words like "mongoloid" and "retarded" to describe my baby. These terms devalued and belittled Heather; she was first and foremost a child of God.

At three months of age, Heather was a smiling baby with a twinkle in her eye—she was very easy to love. But she was often tired and she wasn't gaining weight.

When Bruce and I took her in for a checkup, the doctors detected a heart murmur. After further tests, the cardiologists were called in.

"She needs heart surgery...we'll wait until she's fifteen pounds," they advised.

For the next four months, Bruce and I did our best to help her gain weight. During daily feedings, I would plead with God: "Please help her keep this bottle down." It seemed like such a small request, but each day she would throw up at least one bottle; we never knew which one it would be. I was afraid if she didn't gain weight she would die. Losing Heather was my worst fear.

"I couldn't bear that," I told God.

As the feeding frustrations continued, our doctor decided to do an X ray of her lower abdominal area. It turned out that Heather had a blocked intestine.

Within a few days, our daughter had stomach surgery to repair the problem. After the operation, I felt relieved. "Now she'll be able to gain weight," I told Bruce.

But just a few weeks after Heather's operation, she came down with pneumonia. For weeks, Bruce and I cared for Heather within the confines of a hospital. Night after night, the two of us would keep vigil over her metal crib, watching this little five-pound person struggling for breath surrounded by tubes and bandages and beeping monitors.

"Honey, go home and get some rest," Bruce would say. My husband wanted me to take care of myself. At the time I was pregnant with our second child. Still, I found it hard to leave Heather. I was afraid if I left her side that she would die.

When Heather finally recovered from pneumonia, a team of cardiologists agreed that Heather should stay in the hospital until she had gained enough weight for the surgery.

As our hospital stay wore on, nurses monitored her daily milk intake and recorded weekly changes in her weight.

In between lab work and X rays, Bruce and I would stroll Heather through the halls in a little red hospital wagon.

She was small and weak, but her smile was broad and bright. When she giggled, her whole face lit up. It was hard to believe that her heart wasn't strong enough to sustain life.

When at last Heather hit nine pounds, we met with the cardiologist. "Heather's not going to get any bigger. Let's proceed with surgery," he suggested.

Using diagrams, he explained that a wall needed to be built around a defective chamber in Heather's heart. "To build a wall, I'll need to use existing tissue…some hearts have tissue, some don't," he said.

"Will she make it through the surgery?" Bruce asked.

"I can't give you any guarantees, but I've operated on smaller hearts," he said.

The night before her surgery, Bruce convinced me to go

home and get some rest. "I'll spend the night with the baby," he said.

When I arrived home, I felt exhausted. As I looked at my weary reflection in the bathroom mirror, my eyes began to fill with tears.

"What if Heather dies?" I asked myself.

As I flopped on to the bed, I wanted to deny that Heather's death was a possibility. I didn't have the emotional or physical strength to deal with the loss of another baby. I felt helpless. Death was a distinct possibility. Why wasn't God rescuing her? Why wasn't He protecting her from the pain?

"I'm scared of losing her," I cried out to God.

On my bedside was a Bible. I opened it and began reading: "God is faithful; he will not let you be tempted beyond what you can bear.... He will also provide a way out so that you can stand up under it" (1 Corinthians 10:13).

"But Heather's death is more than I can bear," I prayed aloud.

Soon I felt my body relax as I imagined God welcoming my daughter into heaven. In my mind's eye, I saw a loving Lord tenderly cradling her in strong protective arms.

The image was filled with warmth and comfort. "What if heaven was God's way of rescuing Heather from harm?" I asked myself.

As I thought of Heather in heaven, I knew it would be a gateway to wholeness and healing, a "way out."

In that moment, I realized that God had allowed Heather's weakness for a reason, perhaps to teach me how to rely on the power of God even amid fears of impending death.

"God will be with Heather; God will never leave Bruce and me; God is faithful," I whispered as I fell into a deep and restful sleep.

—◆◆◆—

Now, eighteen years later, as bullets ricocheted over me and Heather and a teenage girl in bib overalls, I repeated those words anew: "God is faithful." I could almost feel God's protective arms around us.

The church grew eerily still. A man yelled from the foyer: "The gunman is down. Everyone out."

Mary Beth and I looked up and saw the gunman slumped on a pew against the wall right behind us.

"Mary Beth, you're hurt," I said. Her shoulder was covered with blood. As Mary Beth ran toward the outstretched arms of help, I sensed she would be okay. She was conscious and talking coherently.

Taking Heather's hand in mine, I turned to reach out for Kim. I gasped; she was lying lifeless on the church pew. "Oh, please God…she's too young…too alive," I told myself. But the reality was, she was gone.

"Everyone out…now!" the loud voice commanded.

In response to his commands, Heather and I ran out to join a dazed and confused congregation. My husband came running toward us. "Are you okay?" he asked. Heather and I were covered with blood from Mary Beth's wound. We must have looked awful.

"We're fine, honey," I assured him. Our other children, Sarah and Doug, came running into our arms. We all crowded around Heather, making sure she hadn't been hurt. It was a moment of great relief. God had protected our family from this evil.

Still, in the midst of my relief, I thought about Kim. She had spent the last minutes of her life praising the Lord. For some reason, I felt assured that God's protection had been with her in death, just as it had been with our family in life.

God had rescued her from harm in a different way by quietly ushering her into the kingdom of heaven. Now Kim was in the loving arms of God who promises to "bear us up" when trials come and to provide a way out when there seems to be none.

As the flashing lights of the paramedics surrounded the church, I readjusted Heather's pink clip.

I wanted to tell her that she was a person of immeasurable value and worth; that someone had taken a bullet for her. I wanted to explain that Mary Beth had shown great love, that she had been willing to give her life so that Heather might live. I wanted Heather to know that God's protection had been with her that night just as it had been so many years earlier.

But as I knelt down so that I could look into her eyes, I knew she wasn't capable of understanding these things.

And so I shared a simpler thought.

"God is faithful, isn't He, Heather?" I said softly.

She nodded as if she understood. "Yes," she said.

A Day Hemmed in Love

*Mema was my dearly loved grandmother. She died over a
decade ago, so my daughters know her mainly through
what I tell them about her. I've shown them many time-
worn photos. They know that Mema had a kind, wrinkled
face. They also know that she tended rosebushes and collected teacups and sewed on an antique sewing machine in
a cellar workshop. They know that she played an important role in my life.*

*"Tell us about Mema and prom day," they are fond of
asking. It's their favorite Mema story.*

I pulled on a string that lit a fluorescent ceiling light and
stood looking around my grandmother's basement workshop. Making my way past a worktable laden with scissors
and spools, I sat down at her cast-iron sewing machine. Above
the machine, a wall plaque read: A Day Hemmed in Love
Rarely Unravels.

It had been a month since my grandmother Mema's death.
In her last moments of life, Mema had wrapped her hands
around mine. Though a cancer was invading her bones, her
brown eyes bore a beautiful sheen, polished from years of
smiling.

"Come back for the sewing machine…it's yours," she had
said.

Now, as I opened the bottom drawer of the sewing machine
cabinet, I found a collection of fabric swatches, saved patches

from treasures that Mema had once sewn for my family.

Although there were piles of gingham and wool and lace squares, a piece of green floral voile caught my eye. As I took the patch into my hand, I forgot that I was a wife and mother of three; now I was seventeen years old, and it was the morning of my senior prom.

Clomping down the stairs that led to Mema's sewing room, my face streaming with exaggerated teenage tears, I plopped my gown on her worktable.

"It looks awful," I wailed.

Mema put on her bifocals, carefully examining the formal I had sewn. The hem was crooked. The waistline was puckering. Threads hung from uneven seams.

Mema shook her head when she saw that I had lined the sheer green flowered bodice with bright yellow satin.

"There wasn't any green lining left; I didn't think the yellow would show through," I whimpered.

"All it needs is the loving touch," Mema said as she held a tape measure to a mismatched sleeve.

For the rest of the day, Mema and I worked side by side at her sewing machine, her shoe tapping the foot pedal as a spool of thread whirled and a needle stitched in a buzz of rhythm.

As Mema mended raveling seams, she reminisced about her past, the hard times of the Depression, losing the farm, the war.

"I sewed your Mom's clothes," Mema remembered.

As I handed her pins, I nodded, but I had heard all the stories before.

Preoccupied with the present, I began to chatter on and on about my date for the prom.

"I think he likes me more than I like him," I admitted.

"Maybe the dress will scare him off," Mema joked. We laughed.

When at last the final seams of the formal were sewn, Mema held the dress up to my shoulders.

"Try it on." She looked hopeful, her brown eyes twinkling.

As I donned the refashioned gown, I danced my way past her sewing machine, my hand grazing the back of my hair like a runway fashion model. Though the yellow lining still didn't quite go with the sheer green florals, Mema's impeccable sewing had transformed my dress into a fashion statement.

"You look beautiful." Mema grinned, her aging face a sweet, unforgettable mixture of crow's-feet and smile wrinkles.

"Love you," I said as I kissed her good-bye and rushed home to get ready for the dance.

That night, my date came to the door with a huge bright pink corsage. He didn't mind that the flowers didn't match my yellow and green gown, he just kept saying how beautiful I looked.

I laughed to myself as I remembered Mema's words, "maybe the dress will scare him off." As we drove to the prom in an expensive limosine, I got up the nerve to tell him I just wanted to be friends.

"That's okay, let's just have fun," he said.

At the dance we mingled with other teenage friends dressed in tuxedos and gowns. We laughed and danced and ate fancy hors d'oeuvres. Everyone told me how funky my dress looked.

Though it was a memorable night, I can't seem to remember what color tux my date wore or where we went to dinner or even where the prom was held. What I do remember about prom day was the special time I spent with Mema. She had given me a memory to tuck away in my heart for a lifetime, like a precious patch of fabric saved for years in a drawer. I would never forget the laughter we shared, the stories I heard, or the age-old wisdom that had rescued me from certain dress disaster. Her presence in my young life was a thread of love that would never be broken.

I slipped the prom dress patch into my pocket and lifted the sewing machine from the cabinet, carefully placing it into a case I could carry.

I took one last look around Mema's workshop. I wanted to remember the way it looked: the scissors, the spools, and the plaque on the wall.

I wanted to remember A Day Hemmed in Love Rarely Unravels.

FAITH IS...

For the past four years, I have run a Sunday school pro-
gram at our church. About a year ago, a young mother
arrived to register her three-year-old son for classes.
Wearing a head bandanna, she explained that she was
receiving chemotherapy treatments for cancer.

As the months passed, Jane and I became good friends.
She shared her cancer story, but more importantly, she
shared her faith.

As Jane tucked her three-year-old son, Bryon, into
bed, she studied a picture that hung on his wall, a
picture of Jesus haloed in rays of light. After the little
boy recited his bedtime prayers, he tugged on his mother's
arms.

"Mommy...what is faith?" he asked.

Jane brushed her hand against his face. Lately she had
talked a lot about faith with her husband, Joe, and also with
family and friends. He must have overheard those conversations.

"Faith is..." Jane said softly. How could she define faith? As
she tried to think of a simple image that Bryon could understand, she couldn't help but reflect on the "faith lessons" she
had recently learned.

As she pulled a blanket over her son's small shoulders, she
remembered a morning just ten months earlier.

She sat in a doctor's office next to Joe while a surgeon reviewed her biopsy report.

"I'm sorry. You have breast cancer," the doctor told Jane as he folded his hands over her chart.

Dressed in a long white coat, he drew diagrams of her surgery options. Jane nodded as he explained about further treatments of chemotherapy and radiation.

She tried to listen to his medical explanations, but an emotional darkness was dimming her capacity to process information. She was paralyzed with fear.

"Any questions?" the surgeon asked.

"I'm sorry," Jane answered. "I have a master's degree but I don't understand a word you've said."

Jane knew he could never answer the real questions:

"Am I going to die?"

"Who will care for Bryon and baby Eric when I'm sick?"

"Who will clean the house, do the wash, make dinner?"

"What does the future hold?"

Jane wanted to sense God's presence; she wanted a miraculous healing. All she felt was the warmth of Joe's hand wrapped tightly around hers.

"We'll get through this," he told her.

Over the next six weeks, Jane underwent surgery and began a regimen of chemotherapy to treat a stage two cancer with lymph node involvement. During this time, it was hard to get out of bed; most days she felt fatigued. It was also hard to look at herself in the mirror. At thirty-eight years of age, she was losing her hair.

"Where are you, God?" she would ask as she cowered over the kitchen sink, trying to control another bout of vomiting.

God never answered her. Jane began to lose faith. As she struggled to manage the unexpected changes in her life, loved ones arrived to help her through this time of uncertainty.

Many afternoons, as Jane rested in her shade-drawn bedroom, she would hear the sound of Bryon's laughter in the living room. Each day, Jane's mother would care for her children, playing games of tag and hide-and-seek.

Sometimes as Jane napped, she would hear the whir of the vacuum as her sister cleaned, or the chopping of a carrot as a friend made soup.

Though she was too weak to get up, the sound of the doorbell ringing always brought Jane great comfort. She knew that a card or a meal or a carefully chosen gift was being dropped off.

Even in the middle of the night, when despair seemed to be strongest, Joe would hold Jane for hours at a time. "Hold on to your faith," he would say as a candle flickered at their bedside.

When at last Jane had completed six months of chemo, she got a three-week break before starting radiation.

Not wanting to waste this short time of reprieve, Jane went on a retreat for those facing life-threatening disease. At the beginning of the retreat, the facilitator asked each participant to take some quiet time of reflection.

"Think about how God has been present in your life," the facilitator said.

Jane closed her eyes. She began to think about all the ways family and friends had cared for her in a time of great need. Their gestures of love had been like soft rays of light shining in the darkness of a debilitating illness. They had been the bearers of Christ's light, holding high the torch of faith, illuminating her cancer path with rays of hope.

She remembered a Bible passage she had memorized as a child: "I am the light of the world," she whispered. Jane knew that Christ, the light of the world, had come to her, not in a miraculous healing, but in the enduring support of loved ones.

"Jesus, strengthen my faith," Jane prayed.

A few days later, Jane began the first of thirty-three scheduled radiation sessions. Though the treatments left her feeling tired, she no longer felt nauseated; this was a blessing she hadn't counted on.

Grateful that the side effects of her radiation were manageable, she began to exercise regularly, walking through her neighborhood a half hour a day.

One afternoon, as she walked through a park, she stopped at a bench to rest. Feeling the warmth of the sun on her face, a great calm came over her.

"I am loved by God," Jane told herself. For the first time in her life, she allowed herself to feel, really feel the power of this simple truth. She had never known such peace.

Throughout the rest of her treatments, whenever she would feel herself sinking into the gloom of doubt and fear, she would remind herself: "I am loved by God…the light of the world is shining on me."

The words gave her strength to go on.

When the day of her last radiation session arrived, Jane and Joe met with the surgeon. "You have an 80 percent survival rate," he reported.

Though the treatments had been aggressive, the doctors could not assure her that the cancer had been cured.

"Technically, though, you're in remission," the doctor said.

Still, Jane felt strangely at ease. She had learned the value of living one day at a time; she had learned to place every hour, every minute, every precious second into the outstretched arms of God.

Now as Jane tucked her young son into bed, she found herself searching for simple words to describe all that she had discovered.

"Faith is…" she repeated.

Maybe she could tell Bryon that faith is believing that sometimes God speaks in strange ways—in the whir of a vacuum or the ring of a doorbell or the smell of chicken soup cooking on the kitchen stove.

Perhaps she might say that faith is the unspeakable comfort of a devoted husband who holds his despairing wife. Or maybe she could explain that faith is the peace that comes when someone finally discovers just how much God loves her.

She could tell Bryon all these things, but she wasn't sure he would understand.

"Faith is a light that never stops shining," she said at last.

As Jane turned her gaze toward the picture that hung above the dresser, Bryon followed her glance.

"Just like Jesus, Mommy?" he asked.

The young mother kissed him on the cheek and slowly dimmed the light.

"Just like Jesus," she whispered.

The Truest of Friends

"There was an immediate bond of love between them, and they became the best of friends" (1 Samuel 18:1, NLT). Every time I read this passage, I think of Sarah, my oldest daughter and her special friend, Maranda. Theirs is a rare bond and is a reminder that love is at the heart of every true friendship.

I pulled the pink envelope from our mailbox just as my daughter was coming home from school. It looked like a birthday party invitation. SARAH was carefully printed in bold, black letters. When Sarah stepped off the bus, I tucked the envelope into her hand. "It's…it's…for me," she stuttered, delighted.

In the unseasonably warm February sun we sat down on the front porch. As I helped her open the envelope, I wondered who had sent it. Maybe Emily or perhaps Michael, pals from her special education class.

"It's…it's…from Maranda!" Sarah said, pointing to the front of the card. There, framed with hearts, was a photo of a girl I had never seen before. She had beautiful long hair, a dimpled grin, and warm, smiling eyes. "Maranda is eight years old," the caption read. "Come and celebrate on Valentine's Day."

Glancing at the picture, I felt uneasy. Clearly, Maranda was not handicapped. Sarah, on the other hand, had Down's syndrome and was developmentally delayed in all areas. At age nine she still functioned on a preschool level. Her disability was obvious, marked with thick-lensed glasses, a hearing aid, and stuttering.

A happy child, she had many friends who used wheelchairs and braces and walkers. But this was the first time she had been invited to the home of a nondisabled child. "How did you meet Maranda?" I asked.

"At…at…school. We eat lunch together every…everyday."

Even though Sarah was in special education, she socialized with other second graders during gym, lunch, and homeroom. I had always hoped she would make friends outside her program. Why, then, did I feel apprehensive?

Because I'm her mother, I thought. I loved Sarah. I wanted and prayed that she would have the best. I also knew a friendship with Sarah called for extra sensitivity, tolerance, and understanding. Was the child in the photo capable of that?

Valentine's Day came. Sarah dressed in her favorite pink lace dress and white patent leather shoes. As we drove to Maranda's party she sat next to me in the front seat, clutching the Barbie doll she had wrapped with Winnie the Pooh paper and masking tape. "I…I'm so excited," she said.

I smiled, but deep inside I felt hesitant. There would be other children at the party. Would they tease Sarah? Would Maranda be embarrassed in front of her other friends? *Please, Lord,* I prayed, *don't let Sarah get hurt.*

I pulled into the driveway of a house decorated with silver heart-shaped balloons. Waiting at the front door was a little girl in a red sweater trimmed with ribboned hearts. It was Maranda. "Sarah's here!" she called. Racing to our car, she welcomed my daughter with a wraparound hug. Soon seven giggling girls followed Maranda's lead, welcoming Sarah with smiles.

"Bye, Mom," Sarah said, waving as she and the others ran laughing into the house. Maranda's mother, Mary, greeted me at my rolled-down car window.

"Thanks for bringing Sarah," she said. "Maranda is so excited Sarah could come to her party." Mary went on to explain that her daughter was an only child and that Maranda and Sarah had become special friends at school. "Maranda talks about her all the time," she said.

I drove away, amazed. Still, I couldn't get over my uneasiness. Could this friendship ever be equal? Maranda would need to learn the language of Sarah's speech. She would need patience when Sarah struggled with certain tasks. That was a lot to ask of an eight-year-old.

As the months passed I watched the girls' friendship grow. They spent many hours together in our home. Fixing dinner in the kitchen, I heard giggles fill the family room as they twirled around an old recliner or watched *The Lion King*. Other times they dressed up in my old hats and outdated blouses, pretending to be famous singers. Soon the months turned to years.

One afternoon in late autumn, 1995, I watched the two of them sitting next to each other at our kitchen table. Sarah held a pencil; Maranda had a tablet of paper.

Maranda called out each letter as she guided Sarah's hand: S-A-R-A-H. Though some of the letters had been printed backward or upside down, Maranda praised Sarah's effort. "Great job," she said, applauding.

At Christmas time the girls exchanged gifts. Sarah gave Maranda a photo of herself, a framed first communion picture. "You look beautiful," Maranda said as she admired Sarah's white ruffled dress and long lace veil. In return, Maranda gave Sarah a gray flannel elephant trimmed with an I love you tag. It quickly became Sarah's favorite stuffed animal, and she slept with it every night.

A few weeks into the new year Sarah came home from school looking downcast. "M-Maranda is...is sick," she said. I thought maybe she had caught the bug circulating at school. A little later, however, Sarah's special education teacher called.

Maranda was in the hospital. She had sustained a seizure at school and had been diagnosed with a brain tumor. Surgeons had performed a risky operation, which had left Maranda paralyzed on one side with impaired speech and vision. The biopsy results weren't back yet.

"Can we visit her?" I asked. I knew Sarah would want to see her friend.

"Maranda is very despondent and not up to seeing anybody," the teacher told me. "Her parents are requesting cards rather than visits."

"We'll keep her in our prayers," I promised.

That night Sarah knelt beside her bed, clutching her stuffed elephant. "Please ma...ma...make Maranda better," she prayed. Night after night she implored God to heal her friend. Then one night in early February Sarah stopped abruptly in the middle of her prayer. She nudged me.

"Let's ma...ma...make a valentine for Ma...Maranda."

The next day we sat together at the kitchen table as I helped Sarah write Maranda's name on a large sheet of pink-and-white construction paper. She decorated each letter with stickers and glittery Magic Markers. She drew a large heart around the name, then glued on candy hearts with phrases like "friends forever" and "be mine." In similar fashion she added four more pages. Just before we slid the card into a large envelope, Sarah asked, "How...how...how do I spell *love*?" I called out the letters as she painstakingly printed LOVE, the letters crooked and out of place, followed by her name.

Two weeks passed. We heard that Maranda had additional surgery. On Valentine's Day I got a phone call from her mother. "Maranda's home," she said, "and wants to see Sarah."

"Home?" I asked with surprise.

"Maranda's tumor was benign. We're hoping for a full recovery."

As we discussed Maranda's prognosis, she relayed how

thankful she was for Sarah and her card. "Maranda was very depressed. She had stacks of letters, cards, and gifts, but wouldn't open any of them. Then one morning Sarah's home-made card arrived. We opened it and Maranda burst into a huge smile. She hugged it and wouldn't put it down." Mary's voice was choked with emotion. "It was an answer to prayer," she said.

I realized then that Sarah and Maranda were the truest of friends. Their bond was defined not by intellect or health or handicap, but by love, unconditionally given and received. They had overcome disability with laughter and support. Their friendship had always been equal.

Today both girls are doing well. Maranda is almost fifteen and Sarah is going on sixteen. With the help of intensive ther-apy, Maranda's neurological functions returned to normal, and Sarah's speech has improved immensely. She can even read some. Though we've moved to a different neighborhood, the girls still keep in touch. Recently Maranda came to sleep over.

As the girls sat at our kitchen table, they talked about Maranda's newly pierced ears and Sarah's "secret" boyfriend from her special ed class. Then in the middle of their conversa-tion Sarah opened a kitchen drawer and pulled out a tablet and pencil.

"S-A-R-A-H," Maranda called out, just like old times. As Sarah printed her name without any help, Maranda looked on and clapped. "Great job, Sarah!" she said. I took a peek at my daughter's masterpiece. She had written her name perfectly.

WILL WORK FOR FOOD

"God did not send his Son into the world to condemn the world, but to save the world through him" (John 3:17). Every once in a while, God reminds me of these words.

Waiting in my minivan at the busy stoplight, my kids and I noticed a bearded man standing on the side of the road. Wearing tattered jeans and a dirty jacket, the man held a sign that read: Will work for food. God bless you.

As we waited for the light to change, my three young daughters stared at him from the back seat.

"Why doesn't anyone help him?" they asked.

I didn't know what to say. I'd read articles about people like him, "modern day beggars who prey on the sympathies of others."

"He *could* find a job," I told myself.

Still, as we drove away, the God voice in my heart began to speak: "I created him, he has a place, a purpose in My kingdom," the voice reminded me.

"Let's pray for him," I suggested, my words hinting obligation.

In my rearview mirror, I watched my daughters fold their hands and close their eyes. "God bless him," they dutifully prayed.

A few weeks later, the kids and I found ourselves waiting in the van at the same busy intersection. Once more, we saw the unkempt man, standing on the curb, holding his sign.

Waiting for the light to change, we noticed a young well-dressed businessman seated in a shiny black Honda; his car was idling right in front of ours. Rolling down his car window, the well-groomed man handed the beggar a loaf of bread and a carton of milk.

"God bless you too," the businessman called out as the light changed to green and he drove away.

As I steered my car toward home, I couldn't stop thinking about the man in the Honda. Somehow, he had found the grace to surrender his assumptions and suspicions, choosing instead to acknowledge and respect a scruffy street-side stranger.

I saw that I had judged the scruffy, jobless man. Through this gift of food and drink, God had answered my children's prayer.

Now every time the kids and I drive past that intersection, we make a point to pray for the bearded man who still keeps his curbside vigil.

A Serenade
of Perfection

A couple of summers ago, my family and I attended a week-long camp for families with a disabled member. During a small group discussion, I met Amy. Like me, Amy was the mother of a handicapped child. In one of our conversations, Amy shared her story of struggle and surrender, and how her faith was sustained and strengthened.

Amy remembers the exact moment God planted the dream. It was a sunny spring morning in rural Wisconsin. Only six years old, Amy sat with her family in the small country church where they worshiped each Sunday.

As the tiny congregation began to sing "Amazing Grace," music from an old pipe organ echoed against the stained-glass windows.

Amy listened as her mother's soprano voice blended in harmony with her father's deep baritone. She closed her eyes. It was a serenade of perfection, an impeccable symphony of song. "I want to sing like they do," she prayed.

When Amy was older, she and her three sisters sang in a church quartet. "Great Is Thy Faithfulness" was one of the songs she loved to perform.

In front of a clapping audience, Amy's voice melted into

flawless melody. *Sounds perfect,* she thought.

By the time Amy started high school, she was taking voice lessons from a teacher who drilled her in repetitions of rhythm, verse, and tone. He expected excellence. Amy dreamed of becoming a professional singer.

But in Amy's first semester of college, she drifted away from the faith she had learned from her family. Pregnant at eighteen, she left school to prepare for both a wedding and a birth.

Amy found herself fighting off a deep sadness. Though Bryan her fiancé was supportive, and she knew God's forgiveness was there to claim, she was overwhelmed with the changes that had come to her life.

Youthful visions were fading fast, replaced now by new and unexpected responsibilities. Instead of pursuing her singing dreams, she was asking: "How can I be a good mother at such a young age?"

In the fourth month of Amy's pregnancy, she felt her baby move for the first time. Wondering if her child might recognize her voice, she began to sing: "Amazing grace, how sweet the sound, that saved a wretch like me…"

Each day Amy sang to her baby, and as her stomach grew in size, she found herself wishing for a daughter. Often she would visualize a pretty little girl with long blond hair and blue eyes. "She'll be smart, the best in her class, a straight-A student," Amy told herself.

She wondered if her daughter would play the same sports she had—basketball and volleyball. But above all these dreams, Amy wanted her daughter to sing. She could almost hear the sweetness of her little girl's voice blending in perfect harmony with hers. *We'll perform together,* Amy thought.

But nine weeks before her due date, Amy went into labor. With Bryan at her hospital bedside, Amy gave birth to a daughter. They named her Leah.

The doctors told the new parents to expect a few hearing

and eye problems, but these concerns would soon prove to be the least of their worries.

At four months of age, Amy noticed that Leah wasn't reaching for toys and that her little body seemed rigid and stiff. Something just wasn't right. After visiting doctor after doctor, the diagnosis came: Leah had cerebral palsy.

Over the next year, Bryan and Amy were propelled into a whirlwind of surgeries and therapies and specialized equipment. Would their baby walk or speak or play? None of the doctors knew for sure.

"Why have you allowed this," she cried out to God.

She was too young for the responsibilities of caring for a handicapped child; she hadn't planned on raising a child with so many needs.

Like every parent, she had hoped for a perfect child. Secretly she felt resentful.

Not wanting to burden Bryan with her bitter feelings, she paid sixty dollars for one session with a counselor. "I don't know why God let this happen," she told the therapist. The counselor only nodded—Amy knew he didn't understand.

Finally, Amy called an aunt who had mentored her throughout the years in areas of faith. Amy's aunt was wise. She often spent time praying and meditating on God's Word. "Why me?" she asked her aunt.

"Maybe God sent Leah for a reason…maybe your daughter is showing you how to surrender your own need to be perfect…"

That night, Amy told Bryan about the conversation she had had with her aunt.

"We are imperfect, just like Leah," Bryan said.

"And God still loves us," Amy added.

The next Sunday at church, Amy and Bryan recommitted their lives to God. Their uncertain future, even their waning hopes and dreams—they surrendered it all to God.

In the months that followed, Amy found comfort in the old songs and hymns she had learned as a child.

One day, as she drove Leah to therapy, Amy began to sing aloud: "Amazing grace, how sweet the sound."

To Amy's surprise her smiling one-year-old bobbed her head up and down as if she was trying to follow the beat of the song.

Later that night, as Amy rocked Leah to sleep, the young mother continued to sing the lyrics of the song, like a lullaby. "I once was lost, but now am found, was blind but now I see."

Leah's spastic muscles began to relax.

Throughout the next ten years, Amy continued to guide her disabled daughter in repetitions of verse and rhythm and tone. Sometimes as she made lunch for Leah in the kitchen, Amy would set a tape player on the counter and play popular children's songs.

"Turn it up," Leah would say as she sang the lyrics way too fast or clapped out of time. Amy was proud of Leah's progress, but voices from the past kept reminding her that the melody needed to sound perfect. She knew God was telling her to let go of the past. Still, she felt disheartened.

"We'll never perform together," Amy told herself.

When Leah turned thirteen, Bryan and Amy took her to a week-long retreat for families of the disabled. One of the retreat evenings was set aside for entertainment; Leah signed up to perform.

On a stage, in front of seventy-five families, the young girl sang "Amazing Grace," proudly holding a microphone from her wheelchair.

From the front row of folding chairs, Amy looked on with a twinge of envy—another mother from the retreat was singing with Leah.

With a soft guitar providing background music, Amy listened carefully to the performing twosome.

Through many dangers, toils and snares
I have already come.
'Twas grace that brought me safe thus far,
And grace will lead me home.

This mother had a beautiful soprano voice. Leah's voice, in comparison, was low and flat and out of tune. Yet as Amy listened, she realized their voices were melding together in poignant praise.

Amy looked around her in wide-eyed silence. She saw teenagers bowing their heads in prayer. She saw parents discreetly wiping away tears.

After all these years of challenge, Amy couldn't believe that she was thanking God for Leah's limitations.

Though it was obvious that her daughter's performance was flawed and unpolished, the Spirit of God was working through Leah's weakness, providing a powerful balance of harmony.

It was a harmony that could bless hearts and touch souls in a way that a perfectly orchestrated song never could.

"Lord, I want to sing with Leah," Amy prayed as she stood and applauded her daughter's performance.

Today Amy and Leah have a mother-daughter singing ministry. The duet has sung together at weddings and baptisms and banquets, offering comfort and support to thousands of listeners across the country.

They sing spirited versions of "Great Is Thy Faithfulness" and "Amazing Grace," along with contemporary songs of hope and praise. Their voices always blend in a beautiful serenade of God's perfection.

Before every performance, Amy and Leah happily remind their listening audience of a lesson they have learned well: "It's okay not to be perfect."

BOOK FAIR BARGAIN

Love. Unselfish, unconditional, uncomplicated. One day last fall as I worked at a school book fair, a little boy taught me something about this kind of love. I didn't catch his name, but I haven't forgotten what I learned from him.

That morning, the school gym had been transformed into a fair for the day. Underneath the basketball hoops long tables were packed with videos and colorful brochures. Tall bookshelves held collectible children's classics: *The Berenstein Bears, Arthur Goes to Camp,* and The Babysitter's Club.

I had volunteered to work at the fair as the checkout lady, a last minute favor for my third-grade daughter. My assignment was to run a cash register at a central table. Just minutes before the book fair began, I scribbled out a to-do list on a scrap of paper. My house was a mess, I had deadlines at work, and the car needed repair.

"I'm so busy," I told the other parent volunteers. I wanted everyone to know what a sacrifice I was making.

All morning long the children came in to browse, one class per half hour. I watched young students page through paperbacks and hardbound books covered with glossy paper jackets. One by one, I tallied totals on a calculator, the children handing me checks their parents had written out—checks for ten, twenty, and sometimes even thirty dollars.

Around lunchtime, a classroom of sixth graders arrived. One boy from the class drew near a table adjacent to mine, the bargain table. It was packed with erasers and stickers and pencil boxes, all marked one dollar.

Blue-eyed and freckled, the boy picked up a poster of a race car, a fushia-colored Ferrari set against a metallic black background.

"Wow," he whispered, his eyes wide. For several minutes, he studied the glossy print, admiring every detail.

"It only costs a dollar," I said with a smile.

The boy dug in his pockets, pulling out four quarters. "It's my lunch money," he said. He had no check from his parents.

A bell rang. Though it was time for him to return to his classroom, the boy lingered on, trying to decide if he should buy the poster. Meanwhile, a group of first graders began filtering through the fair.

Soon a tiny boy wearing a Johnny name tag made his way to the bargain table. Standing on his tiptoes, the child caught a glimpse of the poster held by his older classmate.

"Wow," Johnny whispered loudly.

"It's only a dollar," the boy said as he lowered the poster so Johnny could see.

"I don't have any money," said the little boy.

Without hesitation, the older child handed me his four quarters, exact payment for the race car print.

With a grin, he placed the poster in Johnny's hands, rushing off to join his waiting class.

I remembered my morning resentments, how I had begrudged my gift of time, how I had wanted someone to notice my "good deed."

I saw that the most honorable "gifts of goodness" are given in secret. And flow from a humble heart.

A heart that has no need to be recognized.
A heart that sacrifices without a hint of resentment.
A heart that joyfully shares what is hardest to share.

I spent the rest of the day happily performing my checkout lady duties.

I smiled as I tallied totals, talking and joking and reading with the kids. I even bought a bunch of stickers, secretly tucking them into newly bought books.

I forgot about the messy house, the work deadlines, the unrepaired car.

I had better things to do.

DIFFERENT FOR A REASON

Five years ago I was looking for a typist to help me with my writing projects. I found Sue through the local want ads. Over the years, she's proven to be an excellent associate and a wonderful friend.

Last summer as we worked on manuscripts in her home, the skies outside began to fill with storm clouds. "When it's stormy, I always think of Becky," she said. We sat together at her computer as she told me this story.

Tornado watches are a way of life in Minnesota. Often the storms darken up the sky and we get a bit of lightning and thunder, but usually the winds blow over without causing any damage. But every once in a while, funnel clouds form into merciless whirlwinds of destruction.

It was a pleasant August afternoon in 1969. Just seventeen years old, I was vacationing in northern Minnesota with my family. We were staying at a resort that our church owned.

Our cabin was located at the bottom of a hill next to a lake with steep banks. Three other cabins surrounded us. Relatives, eighteen in all, had crowded into two of these cottages. Two other families occupied the other cabin.

The area was lush with grass. There was a dock nearby where a pontoon boat, a speedboat, and a sailboat were anchored. On the hill by the lake there was a large maple tree that had thick branches overhanging the water. On one of the branches was a tire swing. My cousins and I loved to swing out over the lake and drop in.

I had spent most of that sunny summer day boating and waterskiing with my cousins. It felt great for me to be far away from my hometown.

That year I had graduated from high school. It had been a year filled with peer pressure. Though I was a straight-A student, I never felt like I fit in. I had acne and I was known in the popular groups as an honor society nerd: I worked at the bookmobile during my lunch hours. To top it off, my parents didn't have much money and I wore outdated, hand-me-down clothes.

Now the warm lake breezes made all those teenage pressures seem distant. My only goal for the summer was to learn how to slalom on one water ski.

As the late afternoon sun became overcast, my Uncle Terry steered our speedboat toward the shore. I threw a terry cloth cover-up on over my swimsuit. Shivering, I ran toward the cabin as the wind began to blow.

I tasted a spoonful of stew that my mom had simmering on the cabin stove. She had the radio on. As my mom turned the radio dial to a local station, a weather forecaster warned of funnel clouds that were beginning to form in our area.

No one seemed too concerned. "Tornadoes don't usually strike in northern Minnesota," my mom said. I nodded in agreement, saying that our cabin was in a low-lying area, protected by steep embankments.

As my Mom and I looked out the picture window, we watched the wind heave the once calm lake into a sea that swelled with crashing whitecaps. All along the shoreline, the towering birch trees were bending in gusts that whistled and moaned around the cabin.

Just then, my grandmother and the rest of our family

rushed through the front door—they had come from their cabin on the hill. Watching the clouds swirling to the west, they thought our cabin would afford them better protection from the storm.

"We won't get hit," my Aunt Priscilla said. She was surrounded by her three young children and pregnant with her fourth.

As my family members crowded in front of the picture window, Grandma gave us assurances. "God will take care of us," she said.

Grandma told us that she had not been able to sleep the night before. She had spent several hours reading the Bible and praying. Although the storm was raging outside, she seemed to be at peace.

Meanwhile, my mom stood quietly in front of the window, holding one hand over her mouth. I wondered if she was worried about the rest of our family. Minutes earlier my father and oldest brother had driven to the hardware store in town to buy a part for the sailboat. My eight-year-old brother was also gone. He had walked to a candy store just a mile down the road with our cousin.

I was worried too. I wished my family were together. "At least Becky is here," I told myself as I looked toward the kitchen table where my older sister was weaving a hot pad on a small loom.

Becky was mentally challenged. She was a heavyset teenager with short, wiry hair that never seemed combed.

She was a happy girl with a perpetual smile, but she wore a hearing aid and her speech was difficult to understand. When we were children, I was the only person who could understand what she was saying. I became her "interpreter." I sometimes resented that role.

During my early teenage years, I was embarrassed that my sister was "different." On one occasion, Becky had come with me on a group date. As we drove home that evening, Becky began flirting with my boyfriend, saying inappropriate things. After telling my parents about her embarrassing behavior, my mom and dad assured me that she would never have to tag along again.

Though Becky cherished me, I was always self-conscious about her. I wanted her to look normal, to act normal, to be normal. I'd go to great lengths to improve her appearance: I'd fix her hair, help her put on makeup, and make sure that her clothes were put on right.

"Becky, you need to lose weight," I would tell her.

"But I like to eat!" she would answer.

Regardless of what I did, Becky accepted herself. She loved who she was, she was completely satisfied with the way God had made her. There was a part of me that wished I could accept myself as she did.

Sometimes she would walk around the house repeating Scripture passages that she had learned in Sunday school. One of her favorites was: "We are made in the image and likeness of God."

"That's a nice hot pad," I told Becky as the front door of our cabin blew open.

"There's a tornado coming!" our next-door friends yelled as they burst through the front door.

I never saw the tornado. I never heard the tornado. Witnesses would later say that the half-mile wide funnel swept across the lake just in front of our cabin. Powerfully swirling across the shoreline, the tornado suctioned up a great wall of water, pulling our cabin right off its foundation into the lake.

As a mighty mountain of heavy water crashed down on us, our cabin exploded into tiny pieces. I was thrown hundreds of feet out into the debris-ridden lake. I tumbled through the waves, fighting to make my way to the surface, but a strong circular current kept pulling me under.

As the waters roared and whole trees with roots blew over me, believe it or not, I thought about my recent high school graduation. A guest speaker had shared that, with a class size of 750, some of my classmates would surely be killed within five years. At that time, I had told myself that it was unlikely I would die in my youth. I didn't smoke, I didn't drink, I wouldn't be going to Vietnam. Now, as I fought for life, I was sure I would be one of the statistics he was talking about.

"God, save us!" I cried. When I finally surfaced, I clung to a piece of lumber.

It seemed an eternity before the wind began to die down. I began to tread water and look for signs of life. One by one, heads began bobbing up from the waves. I saw my Aunt Priscilla, her seven-year-old son Shane, and my Uncle Terry.

As the waves pounded me toward the shore, I searched for the familiar landscape of trees and cabins, but all I saw was a mound of dirt where a grassy landscape had once been.

Once on shore, I wandered aimlessly. I think I must have been in shock. When I saw my Uncle Terry caring for my little cousin Shane, I went over to them.

"Are you okay?" my uncle asked. I nodded and I offered him the belt from my terry cloth robe to wrap Shane's bleeding foot. Then I offered my robe to wrap around Shane's bleeding forehead. I prayed for him. Then I saw my Aunt Priscilla emerging from the lake and I went to help her. She started crying—not knowing where her husband and two other children were. We would later learn that her youngest daughter had died in the storm.

As more relatives found their way to shore, I looked up and noticed that the sun was shining—it had only been fifteen minutes since the storm had hit.

Still disoriented, I wandered to the top of the hill and viewed the destruction. There were pieces of windows and chunks of cement scattered all over the ground. Shingles and chairs and boards with protruding nails were floating in the water. There was not one birch tree left standing.

Our friends from next door walked up the hill to report that my dad and two brothers were fine and that my mom had just made it to shore.

"What about my grandma?" I asked.

"She didn't make it," one of them said. He went on to mention several people who were still missing.

It occurred to me that no one had mentioned Becky.

"Did she survive?" I asked.

He sadly shook his head. "Your mom and aunts tried to give her mouth to mouth, but..."

I closed my eyes and sighed. "Why am I alive?" I asked myself.

That night, my family and I stayed at the home of a pastor who lived in town. As I lay on the floor in a sleeping bag next to my parents' bed, trying to get some rest, I heard my father sobbing. I found it hard to understand the tragedy that had come to us. In all, seven died, three were members of my family.

I grieved the most for my sister Becky. Why had God taken her? She was so vulnerable. I felt guilty for the way I had treated her in life. I asked God to forgive the resentments I had harbored toward her.

Then a strange thing happened. I heard a tender voice speaking in my heart: "She was made in My image and likeness." In that moment, I imagined my heavyset sister, her hearing aid, her speech impediment, her perpetual smile.

"She loved who she was," I told myself. "And she loved me."

Though my sister's life had been cut short at only nineteen, she had taught me a very important truth. I too was created in God's likeness, despite my acne and unpopularity and self-consciousness.

Becky loved me despite my "disabilities." Though I had

been intolerant, impatient, and critical, she had cherished me nonetheless. She had always seen me as a beautiful creation of God.

Accepting another without regard for fault or weakness is what is most important in a relationship. Becky knew this better than I.

Now thirty-one years later, I am a wife and mother of four. I now have two daughters that are seventeen and nineteen, the ages that Becky and I were when the tornado changed my life. Though my girls sometimes have normal teenage spats, I try to remind them to accept each other despite their differences.

I encourage them to appreciate the short time they will spend together as sisters. "God made each of you different for a reason," I tell them.

ROSY'S MIRACLE

When I was in college, I had a friend who prayed for a large financial miracle. I supported her in those prayers, but secretly I was skeptical that God would provide. Much to my surprise, my friend got her miracle. What she learned from that has affected her life ever since.

I srael. The shiny black letters were set against the bright yellow background of the brochure. It was posted prominently on the bulletin board in Rosy's college cafeteria. With a backpack flung over her shoulder, Rosy scanned the posted ad as she drank coffee from the Styrofoam cup. "Come travel with us… Come see the holy land…" the flyer read. Memories from her childhood came to mind.

She remembered sitting with her family at church when she was ten years old, the pastor showing slides of Israel. Enchanted, she memorized each sacred place; the rough terrain of the Jordan River, the aqua blue of the Mediterranean Sea, the white stones that framed the tomb of Jesus.

"Please, Lord…let me see Israel someday," she had prayed.

The memory quickly faded as the bell for her next class rang. Jotting down the phone number on the brochure, she rushed off to a lecture.

Later that night in her dorm room as she was unable to concentrate on her studies, she held the phone number in her hand. She wanted to call but she knew an international trip was not in her budget. Finances were tight in her family. She was working her way through school, subsidizing financial aid with a meager waitress salary.

She picked up the phone anyway. "It won't hurt to call," she told herself.

A youth pastor answered. He was happy to share the Israel itinerary.

"How much will the trip cost?" she asked.

"A thousand dollars," the pastor replied.

"I'm sorry," she said. "I can't afford it."

"I won't be needing payment until July 1. That will give you three months," he said kindly.

The pastor seemed to sense her disappointment. "Maybe God wants to work a miracle for you. Why don't you pray about it?" he said.

"A miracle," Rosy muttered as she hung up the phone.

She had never thought of asking God for something as big as a miracle.

Her daily prayers had always been generic: "Lord, bless my family...protect my friends...help me with this exam..."

How could she ask God for a thousand dollars? God needed to tend to those whose needs were greater than hers— the poor, the lonely, the starving of the world.

She crumpled the phone number and threw it in the waste-basket. For hours she tried to distract herself with homework, but she kept hearing the pastor's words: *Why don't you pray about it?*

Soon she was on her knees, her head bowed, her hands folded: "Lord, I'm sorry for asking for so much. I know you are busy answering more urgent prayers," she began, "but I'd like to go to Israel."

As the weeks passed, Rosy prayed every night that God would provide a way for her to finance the trip. Though her intercessions were heartfelt, she always apologized for her request.

"Lord, I know this is a lot to ask," she would pray.

The first day of July arrived. Rosy woke up early just as the sun was rising. She was staying at a girlfriend's house in a private room decorated with white linens and a silver wall cross.

Rosy lingered in bed for a while. "It's the last day to turn in money," she told herself.

A Bible lay close by at her bedside. She opened it and began reading a passage from the book of Ezekiel: "I am going to send you to the nation of Israel," the verse proclaimed.

Could the words be meant for her? Rosy closed her eyes. "Lord, give me faith to believe that You can still work a miracle."

Minutes later, her friend knocked on the door. "Let's go out to breakfast," she suggested.

As the two of them drove to a restaurant, her friend pulled into the driveway of a steepled church. "I'll be right back; I've got to drop something off," she told Rosy.

As Rosy waited in the car, she looked toward the garage of the church rectory. Inside, she saw a tall man in a flannel shirt. He was fixing a bicycle. She recognized him. He had often ridden past her college, and they had waved to each other many times.

Leaving the car she walked toward the garage and exchanged small talk with the man. His name was Lenny, and he was a seminarian. He wanted to be a pastor and was living at the church for a year.

His commitment to God had compelled him to live a life of simplicity. He had pared down his possessions, giving his car to a homeless man. He dreamed of serving the poor in a third world country.

"God gives generously so we in turn can do the same," he told Rosy as he oiled the chain of his bike.

Rosy grew quiet.

His simple lifestyle seemed to contradict her fervent prayers for a thousand dollars. Was she wrong in asking God for so much?

"So what are your plans for the rest of the summer?" Lenny asked.

"I think…I'm…going to Israel," Rosy said.

She told him how she had always hoped to see the Holy Land.

"There's a trip scheduled for August. I can't afford it but I've been praying for a miracle," she said.

Lenny gave the tire on his bike a test twirl. "How much do you need?" he asked.

"A thousand dollars," she said.

Lenny smiled.

"You've been praying that God would answer a prayer of yours, and I've been praying that God would answer a prayer of mine."

He explained that he had recently inherited a large sum of money, and that he'd been praying that God would show him what to do with it.

"But last week," he grinned, "I received an additional inheritance of a thousand dollars. Ever since, I've been asking God who it's for."

At first, Rosy didn't understand what he was saying.

"That person is you," Lenny said.

"Me?"

"You!" he nodded.

Minutes later, Lenny handed her a one thousand dollar check dated July 1.

"How should I repay you?" she asked.

Lenny wasn't at all concerned. "Pay it back to someone who needs it more than I do," he said.

So that August, Rosy went to Israel. She hiked along the rocks of the Jordan River, she swam in the cool aqua blue waters of the Mediterranean Sea, and she smelled the fragrant roses that framed the garden tomb of Jesus.

As she trod the homeland of God, she couldn't stop thinking about Lenny's generosity. By sharing an unconditional gift
Lenny had displayed the love of a gracious God who gives
without measure or limits. It was a brand of giving that she
would model for a lifetime.

Twenty years later, Rosy hasn't forgotten her commitment.
Now a wife and mother, she spends her free time working with
the poor, encouraging the lonely, caring for the handicapped.

And whenever she hears of a financial need, she writes out
a check, sending it off without a return address.

As she drops the anonymous gift in the mailbox, she
remembers the words of Lenny, now a missionary to the poor
of the third world: "God gives generously so we can do the
same."

WELCOMING AMY

My good friend Marie works at Crisis Pregnancy Center.
Every couple of months, the two of us meet for lunch. I
always enjoy hearing about Marie's work. She meets some
very special people.

It had been fifteen years since her abortion, but every
Mother's Day, Marie still found herself conversing with a
child she had never held.

"What do you look like? Do you sing in heaven? I sure love
you," she whispered.

Now thirty-five, Marie had directed the Crisis Pregnancy
Center's ministry for five years. She worked there today, even
though it was a Sunday and Mother's Day. Small silver-framed
photos decorated her office; pictures of young mothers and
newborn infants, all giving gentle testimony to life, freely chosen.

She remembered the unborn baby she had carried in her
womb for two and a half months.

When Marie was nineteen years old, she was unmarried
and pregnant. Embarrassed and ashamed of her secret, Marie
had decided not to seek help from her family. "It would dis-
grace us," she thought. She scheduled an abortion.

However, for the next five years, her decision brought her
unending depression and remorse.

Only by grace had Marie found healing at a church that
welcomed her, supporting her through weeks of postabortion

counseling. At this church, she had met countless women like her, who, in a vulnerable moment, had chosen abortion.

With their help, she had learned to balance the horrors of terminating a pregnancy with the relentless forgiveness of God.

"I'll never stop helping others to choose life," Marie promised her baby.

She fingered a silver-framed photo on her desk. The phone rang.

"Happy Mother's Day," Marie greeted the caller. On the other end of the line a woman was crying.

"I need some help," she said.

"I can give that," Marie assured her.

Homeless and four months pregnant, a nineteen-year-old named Amy was calling from a pay phone. The father of her child was a chronic abuser; now he had left her to deal with the pregnancy alone.

"I don't want an abortion, but I don't have another choice," she said.

Marie reached into her purse and pulled out a cross neck-lace. Though it was ornate and much too large to wear, Marie always carried it with her. During her postabortion counseling, it had been given to her by an elderly woman named Hilda.

Though Hilda had had a secret abortion in the 1950s, she had shamelessly offered Marie an invitation to receive the love of God. It was Hilda who had welcomed Marie into the family of faith.

"You do have another choice," Marie told the caller as she clutched the cross. "I'll help you," Marie added.

Continuing to comfort the pregnant woman, Marie gave her reassurances about temporary shelter and medical care.

"Do you have a family?" Marie asked.

Amy had grown up in an abusive home; it was unsafe for her to seek refuge there.

"I have grandparents…but I haven't seen them since I was

two years old," Amy said. "I don't think they would remember me."

Later that evening, while Amy found rest and comfort in a transitional home supervised by center volunteers, Marie called Amy's grandparents. It was a time zone difference—they lived in Hawaii.

"Hello, my name is Marie. I direct a Crisis Pregnancy Center in Minnesota," Marie told Amy's relatives.

As Marie told of Amy's plight, the elderly couple listened carefully and asked questions. Their first concern was for their granddaughter's welfare.

"Is she okay? Is the boyfriend still abusing her? When is the baby due?" they asked.

After a few moments of reflection, Amy's grandparents agreed to take her in. "God is calling us to help her," they told Marie.

Over the next few days, Marie worked out the arrangements for Amy to join her grandparents. She secured a plane ticket to Hawaii from the board of directors at the center. Other ministry volunteers filled a secondhand suitcase with brand new maternity clothes and a layette for the baby. Still another volunteer dropped off a check for twenty-five dollars.

"Give this to Amy," he instructed. "Tell her she can spend it any way she likes."

The day of Amy's departure arrived. At the airport, Marie and Amy waited on the concourse for a plane that would take Amy to her waiting grandparents.

"You've given me the courage to bring my baby into the world," Amy told Marie. "I want to raise my child right."

"God will help you," Marie said.

"God?" Amy's face looked puzzled.

"Yes. God loves you very much," Marie said.

"Me? He loves me?" This was the first time anyone had said this to her.

In the next few minutes, as harried passengers scurried by with luggage, the two women talked of God's power, His forgiveness, His plan for Amy and her baby.

"God is waiting to welcome you into His family," Marie said softly.

Amy nodded. For her, it was a moment of quiet conversion.

As the two women clasped hands to pray, Marie felt the inner nudging of God.

"Why don't you give Amy the cross necklace?" a voice in her heart suggested.

No, Marie thought. *Not the necklace.*

But as the airport intercom summoned passengers to a plane bound for Hawaii, Marie reached into her purse and placed the cross in Amy's hand.

Amy's face beamed. Marie watched as the young teenage mother put the necklace on over her brand new maternity top.

"This will be the first thing my baby wears," she said as she gave Marie one last hug.

As Amy made her way toward the plane, Marie prayed that Hilda's cross would sustain the young mother through all the uncertain days ahead; that it would always remind Amy that she was now a loved member of God's family.

"Family," Marie whispered as she wondered how Amy would recognize the grandparents she hadn't seen in years.

Just before Amy disappeared down the concourse, Marie called out to her:

"How will you know your grandparents?"

Amy turned around, one of her hands clutching the cross hanging around her neck. Her face was full of joy as she called back: "They told me to look for a WELCOME, AMY sign!"

"I'll Always Be There for You"

"There can be no situation in life in which the conversation of my dear sister will not administer some comfort to me." These are the words of Lady Montagu. Sisters do indeed have a special bond. A few years ago, on a Thanksgiving morning, my sister Annie and I saw a wonderful example of how strong that bond can be.

When I walked into church that Thanksgiving morning, I saw my sister Annie sitting alone in a pew, third row from the back. With a few minutes left before the service, our eyes met, but Annie turned away.

Over the years, we had always been close. As children, we had shared bunk beds and clothes and late night chats. We had always been each other's best friend.

But now that we were both in our late thirties, I a wife and mother, and Annie a single businesswoman, our relationship felt strained.

For the last few months, Annie had been traveling with her job and she rarely had time to visit me.

Though Annie did her best to call regularly, I still felt resentful, even a little jealous. Annie wore expensive suits and dined in fine restaurants and had her nails done once a week at a salon. I, on the other hand, wore budget sweats and tennis shoes; my daily routine revolved around three young children, a husband, and a home in the suburbs.

Just the night before, Annie had stopped by my house to give me a Thanksgiving card. I was grateful for her company, but found it hard to disguise my resentment. As the night wore on, I offered my unsuspecting sister a series of uncalled-for reprimands. "You work too many hours… Get yourself on a budget… Quit smoking, it's bad for you." When I mentioned that I didn't care for Annie's boyfriend, Annie's face had grown red with anger.

"That's it!" Annie had said as she huffed out, slamming the door behind her.

Now I wanted to find a way to say I was sorry. But I wasn't sure Annie was ready to receive my words of remorse.

So instead of joining Annie, I made my way to the back of the church where there was a furnished lobby. I sat down on a floral chair. I happened to notice two women chatting on a nearby couch.

The youngest of the women was in her early thirties. She wore a trendy pantsuit and stylish long hair; a baby slept in her arms. The older was dressed in a navy blue suit trimmed with a silver brooch. I guessed they were sisters; both had identical cheekbones and the same shade of hazel eyes.

"The MS is getting harder to manage," I overheard the younger sister say as she rocked her baby with shaking hands.

I pretended I wasn't listening as the two continued to discuss the disabling disease that often affects the young.

"I'll always be here for you," said the woman in navy blue.

The church organist began to play an opening hymn. The tremoring mother placed her child into the arms of her sister and reached for a cane that rested at her feet. She took a moment to steady herself.

As the two of them linked arms, they slowly shuffled into church, their burdened steps awkward and mismatched.

I lingered behind at a short distance, watching them make their way to two empty places right behind Annie. I wished that I could link arms with my sister, wished that I could take back all the unsolicited comments I'd lashed out with the night before. I yearned for another chance to be supportive.

When an usher noticed me standing at the back of the church, he motioned for me to take a place right beside the woman with the cane. With the Thanksgiving holiday, the church was crowded; it was the only seat left.

I sat down. I was close enough to touch Annie's back. But I didn't.

"We gather together to sing the Lord's praises," the congregation sang. The woman with multiple sclerosis reached for a hymnal. Though she tried to keep a firm grip on the book, it fell to the floor.

Nonetheless, the sisterly pair clutched hands and sang aloud: "He chastens and hastens, His will to make known."

"Today let us take a few moments to thank God for the blessings He has shown," the pastor said.

As the afflicted mother began to lower herself to kneel, she fumbled for balance. Even though the older sister cradled the baby, she stretched out a free arm to protect her sibling from a fall. I turned my glance toward Annie. I wanted my sister to turn around. I wanted to see her face. I prayed asking God, "Please forgive the bitterness of my heart."

In directing envy toward Annie, I saw that I had neglected the blessings God had bestowed on *my* life. The gift of motherhood, a husband, and just enough money to enjoy life were more than cause for praise. As I continued to pray, I was also aware that Annie's enduring presence had brought immeasurable joy to my life. Our bond would also remain unshakable even if one of us couldn't walk or hold a songbook or kneel without stumbling. Surely Annie and I could shuffle through the changes that had come into our lives recently.

As the church service ended with a song of Thanksgiving, I tapped Annie on the shoulder. "I'll always be there for you," I whispered. Annie turned around and reached for my hand.

"Me too," she said.

"TAKE WHAT YOU NEED"

My Uncle Franny grew up during the Great Depression. He remembers that era as a time when people of "means" gave freely to those in need.

Now in his retirement, my uncle is spending his days managing a ministry which bridges the gap between the "haves" and the "have nots." Here he recounts the humble beginnings of a charity that now serves thousands of needy families.

A t fifty-eight, life had been good to me. I'd been happily married to Jeanne for thirty-seven years. Together we had raised seven great kids. Throughout the decades, my landscaping business thrived; I had made and saved good money, enough to pay off the house, enough to live comfortably for years to come.

Still, the thought of early retirement left me feeling uneasy. What would I do with all my time?

I wasn't the type to play golf or work crossword puzzles, and I couldn't imagine myself watching TV for hours on end.

"It's payback time," I told myself. "Time to thank God for all the blessings I've been given, time to help others in need."

Maybe that's why I took the janitor job at our church. It was a large suburban parish, and I figured I might meet someone who was down on their luck. *Maybe I could offer some quiet assistance,* I thought.

But as I scrubbed floors and cleaned toilets, I didn't meet

anyone who needed my help, just a lot of friendly folks who served on church councils and committees. Soon I became known around the church as "Good Ole Fran, the maintenance man."

All the attention was nice, but each afternoon after my work was done, I would slip away to a back row pew. There I would kneel, fold my hands, and pray: "Lord, show me those in need."

Then one Monday morning as I was cleaning up after a weekend retreat, I noticed an unassembled crib leaning against the church entryway.

I scratched my head. Why was the crib there? I assumed someone had donated it.

Within an hour, I was helping a worker from Catholic Charities load the crib into the back of a truck.

"We've been praying for a crib," the worker said as he slid the mattress into the back of his pickup. "Just yesterday, an unwed mother called. She's got a subsidized apartment but not even one piece of furniture," he added.

As the truck drove away, I couldn't stop thinking about that pregnant girl. Without furniture, she was probably sleeping on the floor.

The thought brought back childhood memories of the Great Depression. Back then I was just a boy and my family was poor, very poor.

All seven of us lived in a small three-room bungalow that had no running water; we used an outhouse for a bathroom. Mom sewed our clothes from old castoffs and my brothers and I slept on thin feather-tick cushions that covered our attic floor. Night after night, as I lay upon the cold floorboards, I would dream about falling asleep on a comfy mattress with warm blankets and pillows.

"No one should have to sleep on the floor," I told myself as I made my way back into the church.

Later that afternoon as I was cleaning the church kitchen, Father Tim, the pastor, rushed past me on his way to do hospital visits.

"Hey, Tim," I called out. "I need to place an ad in the Sunday bulletin. I'm collecting used furniture and clothing for the poor."

Father Tim stopped. He grinned quizzically. "Are you starting a ministry, Fran?"

"A ministry?" I wasn't even sure what a ministry was. "Naw. I'm not starting a ministry. I'm just helping the poor."

Soon word spread that Good Ole Fran was collecting household stuff for the needy. Within a week, our home garage was packed with assorted furniture of all sizes and shapes and conditions, plus household items of every description.

The donations kept coming as my wife, Jeanne, began answering our phone thirty to forty times a day and sometimes during the night.

Each caller expressed a simple but desperate need:

"Is this the man who gives away beds?"

"Does your free store have any warm blankets?"

"Do you carry warm winter coats for children?"

There were times when Jeanne would greet me after work with numerous addresses she had jotted down. I, in turn, would load the donations into the back of an old beatup truck that had once been a dirt hauler for my landscaping business. Then I would deliver what I could to each address.

Before long, we had organized a group of volunteers from the church to help us.

"We can help sort and fold clothes," said two silver-haired seniors.

"I can help Jeanne with phone calls," offered a single mom.

"We'll pick up and deliver donations," said a couple of young fathers.

One night, as the volunteers met in my home, a briefcased

businessman asked: "What do we call ourselves?"

I closed my eyes. Soon I imagined a small bridge arching over raging waters. On one side of the bridge stood a gathering of people, their faces were downcast, their lives had seen nothing but poverty and disappointment.

On the other side stood another group. Their lives had known blessing after blessing and their hands were reaching out to help the others cross.

"Bridging!" I said.

The volunteers liked the name. "We'll be a bridge between the 'haves' and the 'have nots,'" I added.

As the months passed, Bridging flourished. With three home garages now filled, parishioners began to drop off donations in the church basement. The parish began to look more like a rummage sale than a tidy worship space.

One morning as I vacuumed, Father Tim tapped me on the shoulder.

"Frannie," he called out, trying to drown out the loud whir of the vacuum.

I turned off the machine.

"Frannie," he continued, looking me right in the eye. "I love what you're doing for the poor, but you gotta get this junk out of here," he said firmly.

It was time to call Howie, my brother-in-law. A successful building contractor, now retired, Howie had a strong business sense that balanced my enthusiasm to help the poor.

"What do I do with all this stuff?" I asked Howie, as I led him through the hallways of the furniture-packed church basement.

"You need a warehouse, Fran," he advised.

By the end of the week, a businessman from the parish had donated a rent-free warehouse to the ministry. "You can use it until I sell it," he offered.

That warehouse was a mess, but Howie and I soon fashioned makeshift tables from discarded barrels and scraps of plywood that lined the concrete storehouse walls. In time, the tables were bulging with pots and pans, pillows and sheets, dishes and blankets and towels. Howie even rigged up some sturdy scaffolding to hold mattresses and cumbersome pieces of furniture.

The donations kept coming. Volunteers multiplied. We drafted weekly schedules for truck drivers and merchandise sorters, and I finally made arrangements to leave my janitor job at the church. Somehow I knew that this was my "retirement mission"—to care for the poor.

And the needy came to the doors of Bridging.

Some walked just a few blocks. Others took the bus from the inner city. Still others came arm in arm with a social worker, a pastor, or a friend.

"Take what you need and leave the rest for others," I told each person who passed through the warehouse.

Those words seemed to offer comfort as the poor shared their stories:

"Thank you for the beds," one mother of five told me. "Now my children don't have to sleep on the floor."

"Our son is dying of AIDS," an Asian father related. "Now he'll be comfortable in his last days."

"I haven't had sheets or a pillow in years," said a tattered old man with decaying teeth.

So great was the need for mattresses and bedding that sometimes we had to send the poor away from the warehouse without a much-needed bed.

I didn't like doing that.

"No one should have to sleep on the floor," I told Howie one day as I scanned the warehouse scaffolding, now mattressless.

"Fran." Howie winked. "There are lots of mattress stores in town."

Soon the two of us were picking up donated mattresses from a local furniture company, mattresses that the store would have discarded.

Howie and I began stocking the warehouse with twenty to thirty mattresses a week. We never ran out of mattresses again, but sometimes, when bedding would run low, Howie and I would make our way to the local hotels.

"Got any sheets for the poor?" I would ask the hotel receptionist. "How 'bout some pillows?" Howie would add. We were hard to turn down.

Soon the tables were turned and the five-star hotels were calling us.

"Hey, Fran," the hotel managers would say. "We're remodeling; could your ministry use about a hundred sofas?"

Whenever Bridging had a need, it was always met by the generosity of another. Colleges started sending us computers and chairs and desks. Major department stores began delivering semi truckloads of dolls and boots and bikes. Local churches held furniture drives and corporations mailed us gift checks to help subsidize our costs. From shiny new delivery trucks to a couple of unmatched spoons, each offering, great or small, made a difference to Bridging and to the poor we served.

To accommodate the large volume of donations, Bridging moved from warehouse to warehouse—four times in six years. With each move, Bridging gained much-needed space but our monthly rent costs kept rising.

Howie took note.

"Fran," he said one day, as he wrote out a check for warehouse rent. "You need to hire an executive director."

"The good Lord will take care of us," I told him.

"The heck He will," Howie retorted. "You need books and a budget. You need someone to write grants, someone to network with local businesses, someone to record Bridging's yearly growth," he said emphatically.

"And how will Bridging pay for this director's salary?" I asked.

"The good Lord will take care of that," Howie assured.

And the good Lord did take care of that.

Several anonymous grants arrived in the mail that month. We hired our executive director. As a result, Bridging began to establish relationships with Target and Wal-Mart, Gabbert's, Slumberland, and Dayton's (to name a few). With a director now securing financial support from CEOs of foundations and bank presidents, I was freed up to speak at schools, churches, and synagogues.

Though I had never taken a speech course and my grammar wasn't flawless, I found myself speaking confidently in front of hundreds of listeners.

I spoke about Jessica, the little girl who thanked me for a shoebox full of eating utensils. "Now my mom and I don't have to share spoons," Jessica said.

I told them about Tyrone, the shabbily clothed boy who "paid" me for a new bike with two pieces of candy from his pocket.

I told them about Al, an elderly man who eventually became a Bridging volunteer.

"Do something for the poor," I told each audience. "Don't waste your time watching TV. Give what you can to those who have nothing. Bridge the gap between the haves and the have nots," I added.

Soon the local newspapers and TV stations began doing feature stories on Bridging. Though the reporters started calling me The Father Teresa of Minneapolis, I just kept thanking God for answering my prayers. Not only had He shown me the needy, but He had crowned my retirement years with purpose and meaning. I'd never been happier.

Then one night, as I drove home from a speaking engagement, I felt a sharp pain in my chest.

"I just don't feel well," I told Jeanne as I arrived home that night.

A few hours later, emergency room doctors confirmed our

worst fears. I was on the verge of a massive heart attack; 96 percent of one artery was blocked and I would need an immediate quintuple bypass operation.

As I was wheeled into surgery, I made a promise to God. "Lord," I prayed, just seconds before the anesthetic took hold, "if you give me life, I'll never stop serving the poor."

I made good on that promise.

Today I'm stronger than ever, managing a ministry that has gained national support and recognition. Over eighty-nine social agencies rely on the services that Bridging provides. This past year Bridging gave away five thousand beds, two thousand sofas, and six thousand chairs. Four hundred fifty volunteers continue to advance our mission by helping those in need.

It feels great knowing that Bridging has made a difference to so many people, not the least of which is me.

It doesn't matter how old we are; God never stops calling us to help others.

I'm glad He called me. It sure beats doing crossword puzzles.

THE LEAST OF FEET

Many people in the Minneapolis area have heard of Mary Jo Copeland. She runs a large ministry that serves the down and out. When I first visited her inner-city drop-in center, I felt quite uncomfortable. Mary Jo seems to have wonderful rapport with the people she serves. I, on the other hand, found it hard to take the endless stream of people, all with needs for food, clothing, and shelter. It didn't take long for Mary Jo to put me at ease.

I t's a rough part of town," I told myself as I drove into the parking lot of the Minneapolis charity.

That morning, I had come to volunteer for Mary Jo Copeland, the founder of Sharing and Caring Hands, an inner-city ministry that serves twenty thousand people a month.

I had read about Mary Jo in a national magazine. I knew she was in her midfifties, the mother of twelve, and that her charity functioned on a budget of never-ending donations.

I also knew that many in our community called her "a servant of Christ." What did that mean? As a new volunteer, I told myself, I really should know the answer to that one.

As I got out of my van, I locked the doors. I wished my children hadn't piled tennis rackets and broken skates and shopping bags in the back seat of the car. It was obvious I was middle class.

As I walked past a long line of people waiting outside the cafeteria where Mary Jo serves meals, I felt uncomfortable.

Many of the people were unkempt, wearing faces of hope-lessness, all of them carrying something—a backpack, a baby, a Bible.

These were people most of society would shun: a woman with rotting teeth, a crying man with a shaking disease, a teenager who reeked of body odor and cigarettes.

They watched me, and I tried not to make eye contact. It wasn't that I felt better than them; I had known hard financial times but had been spared the pain of hunger and homeless-ness.

"So glad you could come," a nicely dressed woman said as she greeted me at the cafeteria door. Ushering me inside, she assured the waiting crowd that breakfast was almost ready.

I knew the woman was Mary Jo; I recognized her from the magazine pictures I had seen. Her eyes were full of energy and kindness. A barrette was clipped in her hair.

"Can I follow you?" I asked.

She motioned me into the kitchen where a group of volun-teers, uniformed school kids and their parents, were gathered to cook and serve the morning meal.

"Lord, give us your heart of love," Mary Jo prayed as she pulled me into the hand-holding circle. "Bless the poor we serve," she added.

Soon the cafeteria began to swell with over two hundred fifty people.

"C'mon, honey," Mary Jo said as she led me past long tables where the poor ate hot blueberry pancakes and slices of melon.

"Did you get enough to eat? Are you feeling better today? How's the bus driving job?" Mary Jo asked as she shared hand-shakes and hugs.

Her questions set me at ease. She seemed familiar with the people; she knew their stories. I wanted to know them too, but I was hesitant to offer a greeting, some of the people bore expressions of hardness.

"Do you ever have crime here?" I asked.

"Hardly ever. The poor take good care of me." Mary Jo grinned.

From across the room, a tall man in an orange-feathered hat began to sing: "Swing low, sweet chariot…"

Following his lead, a woman in an outdated dress stood up pretending she had a microphone: "Coming for to carry me home…" she sang.

Soon the whole cafeteria was singing and harmonizing: "Swing low, sweet chariot coming for to carry me home."

I couldn't help but join in on the last line.

"Those who would like their feet washed, please join me in the hallway," Mary Jo announced from a loud speaker.

We headed to a corridor framed with cabinets and a sink. There a bearded man in a baseball cap filled up plastic basins with warm, soapy water.

I watched as he carried the basins to the feet of twelve people seated in a circle of folding chairs.

"Is he on staff?" I asked Mary Jo.

"He's homeless; an alcoholic. He fills up the basins every-day," she said.

"Does he drink while he's here?" I asked.

"Never. But I'm sure he drinks at night," she said.

Mary Jo happily shrugged her shoulders: "Jesus never judged, why should I?"

The foot washing began, as the gathered people removed their shoes, their sockless feet now betraying the sores of miles walked in wrong-sized shoes.

Some feet were blistered and swollen, others were ulcer-ated, infection setting in.

As the poor quietly soaked their wounds, Mary Jo made her way around the circle, kneeling before each person with a clean white towel and a tube of soothing lotion.

Wearing latex gloves, she gently massaged their ailing

arches. She talked with them, asking for a name and looking with compassion into a face that needed to be noticed.

I listened in.

Twila was a mother and waitress, heavyset with warm brown eyes. She had fallen behind on her rent payments, the first time in two years according to a stamped letter she handed to Mary Jo.

"Been workin' real hard, but sometimes it ain't enough," Twila said.

"Bob!" Mary Jo hollered as she dried Twila's feet.

A man in a plaid flannel shirt appeared. A volunteer, he held a ledger book.

"Give her $325," she whispered to him. "And throw in a picture of Jesus," she added.

I knew that Mary Jo was the person who heard all requests for aid, that she alone determined who received shoes, bus vouchers, dental care, diapers, even free shelter, whatever the poor needed.

I wondered if anyone ever took advantage of her kindness.

"Do you ever say no?" I asked quietly.

"Every day, but Jesus gives me discernment," she replied, moving on to kneel before a mentally ill man.

Babbling on and on, the dazed man seemed unaware that Mary was soothing his tattered feet with a healing lotion.

"Otis, you sure talk a lot," she said in jest.

"Mary Jo been good to me," he mumbled.

The last to have his feet washed was Brenden, a little boy about six years old.

"Do your toes hurt?" Mary Jo asked as she helped the boy take off his small, unmatched socks.

"Yep," he nodded, blisters blotching his tiny feet.

"This little piggy went to market," Mary Jo joked as she wiggled his big toe in the water.

The boy giggled. As I watched, I thought about my own eight-year-old daughter.

"I need a size five shoe!" Mary Jo shouted.

Taking off her gloves, she helped Brenden lace up his new Adidas. Then she patted his face.

"Take good care of those feet. Someday they'll take you to the kingdom of God."

As I sat there, I remembered a verse from John's Gospel: "[Jesus] poured water into a basin and began to wash his disciples' feet, drying them with the towel" (John 13:5).

Mary Jo was modeling the servanthood of Christ. She humbly and willingly knelt before her brothers and sisters to soothe the sores of the poor with the water of mercy and the towel of tender compassion.

Like Jesus, Mary Jo was a healer of pain, binding the blisters of poverty, hunger, and disease, massaging the wounds of hopelessness and despair.

I no longer felt ill equipped to be a volunteer. Mary Jo had shown me that a servant's love is nothing less than the love of God in us.

Late that afternoon as I walked to my van, I noticed my feet were aching from walking all day.

As I started my car, I slipped off my shoes, suddenly remembering Mary Jo's words: "Take care of those feet. Someday they'll take you to the kingdom of God."

I looked toward Sharing and Caring Hands, and bowed my head in a prayer of gratitude.

My "someday" had already come.

I LOVE YOU MORE

On Thursday mornings I attend a Bible study at a nearby church. There are about ten of us—all different ages and backgrounds. Beverly leads us in prayer and discussion and often shares what God has taught her.

At seventy-seven, Beverly was very careful with her money. She lived in a modest apartment, using coupons for groceries, and she lived frugally.

She rarely splurged on anything for herself. But her bedroom decor was outdated, and she felt it was time for a little change. Maybe that's why she bought the bedspread that day, a costly white coverlet embroidered with delicate ivory roses.

As she smoothed the expensive spread over her bed, carefully tucking and fluffing each edge, she stood back, admiring the transformation in her bedroom.

"It looks elegant," she thought.

The phone rang, startling her.

"Hello, Beverly. It's John." Beverly had been expecting to hear from her former pastor and his wife. Three years earlier she had taken care of their two toddlers. Now the whole family was in town for a three-day visit and they would be staying with her.

"I've got dinner ready for you," she said. "Come over any time."

A little later the pastor's family knocked on Beverly's apartment door.

"So glad to see you," Beverly smiled as she hugged the children: Andrea, five, and Ben, now seven years old.

As Beverly's guests gathered in her kitchen, Beverly poured glasses of grape juice for the children.

The adults exchanged small talk, the pastor sharing stories about his new church.

Soon Andrea and Ben, bored with the adult conversation, slipped away.

The two children began to explore the apartment, making their way into Beverly's bedroom. They squealed with delight as they began jumping on the snow-white spread that covered Beverly's bed.

Then Andrea stopped leaping. "I don't feel too good," she told Ben as undigested grape juice spattered from her mouth, staining Beverly's new coverlet.

"Mommy, Daddy, Beverly; come quick!" Ben shouted, his voice tinged with urgency.

As the grown-ups ran into the room, they discovered not only upset children but Beverly's beautiful white quilt now was a speckled shade of lavender.

Pastor John and his wife apologized. "We're so sorry," they said.

Andrea began to cry.

"Don't be upset," Beverly said softly as she knelt down and brushed the little girl's hair. "I love you more than a silly blanket," she added.

Later that night, after Beverly tucked the children into bed, hugging and kissing each one, she took the spread off of her bed and dabbed each purple stain with cold water.

After washing it, she discovered, much to her amazement, that the stains had completely disappeared. The bed linen was now pure white, as white as when she had bought it.

Once more, Beverly carefully smoothed the coverlet onto her bed and a verse from Matthew came to mind: "You can't serve two masters, God and money, for you will hate one and love the other."

She was grateful that she had learned to live simply, free from the love of high-priced possessions.

She was also thankful that this embroidered spread would never hold more value than her faith in God or the people she loved.

Nonetheless, she grinned as she stood back to admire the freshly washed bed cover.

It still looks elegant, she thought.

A SHEPHERD'S CALL

For centuries, Christians have given their lives in service of the gospel. Though Jim was killed almost twenty years ago, his cousin Jane clearly remembers his well-lived life and the passion for the gospel that compelled him.

It was 5:30 A.M., and a fierce February wind rattled her bedroom window. Jane made her way through the drafty darkness, down the hall to the kitchen.

In another two hours she would need to be at work. A social worker for the elderly, Jane usually found her job at the nursing home rewarding. But today she just didn't want to go in. Lately her clients seemed to have so many overwhelming needs. She wanted a break.

After brewing a cup of steaming hot tea, she curled up on the living room couch, a scrapbook in her lap.

As she turned to the first page, she found a photograph of her cousin Jim, one of her favorites, one of the last ever taken.

In the snapshot, he was standing at the edge of a Guatemalan forest, just a few miles away from the Indian center where he worked. Though he was broad and burly, a man of thirty-seven years, he tenderly cradled a lamb in his arms.

Jane brushed her hand over the picture. It had been eighteen years since Jim's death; he had been gunned down while serving the poor of Central America. "He knew he was going to die. Why did he go back?" Jane asked.

It was a question that often troubled her. Hoping to glean

an answer from her memories, she closed her eyes and thought about Jim's life.

She remembered her cousin as a little boy. He was sitting on the porch of his family's home on a farm in central Wisconsin. With a stack of books piled at his feet, Jane sat next to him, the warm summer sun tanning their seven-year-old faces.

"I'll read to you," Jim told her as he sounded out each word and phrase. Even early on, Jim had the gift for teaching.

Several years later, when Jim was a sophomore at a high school run by the Christian Brothers, Jane chatted with him at a family gathering.

"I'm going to become a missionary," he told her. He went on to explain that a missionary had visited his religion class.

"He showed us slides of a mission school in Central America," Jim went on.

As Jane listened, he repeated statistics he had memorized from the classroom presentation: "Fifty percent of all Central Americans make less than $73 a year, 81 percent of the children suffer from malnutrition, and over half the deaths in Central America are children under the age of four," he said.

Though Jane felt genuine sympathy for the third world poor, she had a hard time taking Jim seriously. "You're going to the jungle?" she giggled in fun. All she could think about was the Tarzan movie she had just seen. The two cousins laughed.

In the summer of 1968, Jim joined the Christian Brothers. Now in his midtwenties, he had completed a degree in Spanish but was still too young to be a missionary. Instead, the Christian Brothers made arrangements for him to teach at a middle-class Catholic school in St. Paul, Minnesota.

Though Jim had hoped for an immediate missionary placement, he reluctantly agreed to the city teaching job. He began his career building the first language lab at the school, while Jane married and settled into a home right down the street from Jim's school.

The two cousins visited often. "How's the job?" Jane would ask as they drank coffee in her kitchen.

"It's giving me good teaching experience," Jim would say.

Jane knew it was second best.

After another two years had passed, Jim received an assignment to work in Nicaragua. Jane hosted a congratulations party in her living room—Jim grinned and laughed and toasted each guest with a glass of punch.

"I'm going to Nicaragua," he said. Jane had never seen him so happy.

During Jim's first year in Nicaragua, he fit right in; he seemed to have an innate understanding of the language and culture. The local people loved him; this jolly, dark-haired man who always smiled.

Still, Jim felt overwhelmed with the needs of the peasants who came to his mission from the hills; most were shabbily clothed and malnourished; nearly all the people were illiterate.

Night after night, Jim would pray beside his bed, asking God to help him build a school. As he waited for God's answer he gained popularity, teaching many people to read and write even without the benefit of a walled classroom.

Soon his name became known in government circles. In time, he was introduced to the Samozas, a wealthy family that controlled much of the government.

"I need money for a school," he told the Samoza cabinet members.

Though Jim was wearing blue jeans and a T-shirt, the well-dressed government officials took a liking to the grinning, gregarious man. In time, he received state-supported funding to build schools to teach carpentry, pipe fitting, mechanics, and welding, ten facilities in all. Some of the schools provided free housing and meals for the students who came from the poverty-stricken hills.

As Jim busied himself with educating the people, a civil war was escalating in the country. Soon the Sandanistas, a powerful Communist group, overthrew the existing Samoza government. Many innocent lives were lost in the battle.

Though Jim's only interest in Central America was to serve and empower the poor, the Sandanistas now identified him with the ousted Samozas.

"I heard gunfire outside my school today," he wrote to Jane. "But I pray better under my bed," he quipped.

In 1979, after spending nine years in Nicaragua, the Christian Brothers summoned Brother James back to the U.S. "It's too dangerous," Jim's superior told him.

When Jim arrived home in St. Paul, he quickly made his way to Jane's house. As he stood in her entryway, Jane's two small children wrapped their arms around the cousin Jane had talked so much about.

"It's good to be home," Jim said as he reached out to hug the kids.

But Jane noticed a deep sadness in his eyes, she knew his heart was still in Central America.

Over the next year, Jim taught Spanish at the middle class school where he had begun his teaching career.

In between classes and working as the school janitor, Jim would walk down to Jane's house to visit, to baby-sit, and even to help with home repairs.

As the two cousins sat on the living room couch, Jim would talk of the high standard of material wealth in America.

"The students here don't understand that education is a gift from God. It's a sin to waste that gift," he told Jane.

Many of Jim's students had parents who were paying expensive tuition for a private education. Jim was frustrated that some of his students were uninterested in learning and unappreciative of their parents' financial sacrifice.

"The Central American people are poor, but they want to learn," Jim said.

As time passed, Jim's smile began to fade. He walked slower and he always seemed down.

"I want to go back to my people," Jim told Jane one day as he ate a sandwich at her kitchen table.

Jane had read about political wars brewing all over Central America. She had heard that missionaries caught in the middle of tensions had been killed.

"It's not safe," Jane replied.

Restless, Jane's cousin found a way to return to the war torn land. Jim agreed to accept a mission assignment in Guatemala, a small country that bordered Nicaragua. "It's safer," Jim's superior told him.

Jane remembered the afternoon her cousin came through the front door waving his official assignment papers. "I'm going back," he exclaimed. His smile, his joy, and his energy had returned.

When Jim first arrived in Guatemala in the winter of 1980, he became an administrator at an Indian center which provided housing and food for one hundred fifty boys, poor peasants from the surrounding mountains. He also taught at the Christian Brothers school located at the edge of town.

When he discovered that there were no textbooks to teach the students about their culture, he immediately began compiling all the literature he could find, organizing and editing where necessary. Soon the children were learning from Jim's makeshift books.

In one letter to Jane, Jim described a homemade textbook he had titled: *Pre-Colombian Art and Civilization.*

"I want the children to learn and be proud of their heritage," Jim wrote.

Though the country of Guatemala was becoming increasingly dangerous, a political war raging between the military government in power and the rebel forces, Jim kept searching for ways to offer his students a better way of life.

Not far from the school, there was a farm that some other missionaries had abandoned. In time, the Christian Brothers took it over, and soon Jim was holding classes there, teaching the boys how to farm the stony mountainous terrain, how to preserve good soil and irrigate the sloping land, how to raise pigs.

One day a lamb wandered onto the farm and one of Jim's coworkers snapped a picture of him cradling the frightened animal. "I'm taking care of a lost lamb," Jim wrote.

Jim came home in late November 1981, on a short winter break.

As he gathered with Jane and her family in her living room, he talked about how unsettled Guatemala was becoming. Associates of his school, friends and family of his staff had disappeared, some had been found tortured and dismembered.

"All the missionaries in the area have made a pact," Jim said firmly as he took Jane's hand. "If the soldiers come for us, we will resist arrest," he went on.

Jim explained that resisting a soldier usually meant certain death.

"It's better to die outright for God than to disappear, never to be found again," Jim reasoned. "We won't put our families through that," he added.

"No, it's better to live for God," Jane said. She understood Jim's passion for the poor. Still, she wanted to remind him that God's work with the poor could be done in America and that he need not give up his life. She didn't want him to go back.

After a holiday celebration at Jane's house, Jim returned to Guatemala on New Year's Day, 1982.

Just six weeks later, as he stood on the sidewalk repairing the outside wall of the Indian center, he was gunned down by three men in military uniforms.

Jane studied the photo of her cousin holding a lamb, a picture that was sent to her by the Christian Brothers two weeks after Jim had died.

Memories of Jim lingered as Jane began to understand in a way she never had before, why he had returned to the dangers of a foreign land far from the comfort of family and the safety of home.

"He was called to be a shepherd," she whispered.

Now it was more clear to her that Jim was on an "assignment from God," called to tend the lost lambs of this earth; the poor, the hungry, the uneducated of the third world.

Like a shepherd Jim guided his flock, his people, to places of shelter, teaching them to read from makeshift books, showing them how to grow crops on a hardened mountain, empowering them with hope by teaching about a God who loves them.

In doing all this, Jim had modeled the love of a humble God who once said: "What do you think? If a man owns a hundred sheep, and one of them wanders away, will he not leave the ninety-nine on the hills and go look for the one that wandered off?"

As Jane's living room began to fill with the first rays of a February dawn, she whispered: "It is good to live for God...it is also good to die for God."

For the first time since Jim's death, she felt an overwhelming sense of peace. "Jim died a happy man. He was doing the work of God; he was taking care of God's lambs," she thought.

"I need to do the work of God too," she said. She thought about her clients. They were her flock. She closed the scrapbook and looked at her watch. "I'd better get going."

CHEERFUL GIVERS

God calls each of us to share our time, talents, and treasures with others who are in need. Sometimes giving can become routine and we forget that sharing a gift should be a great joy.

R obin and Kevin were a young couple working full-time jobs and living on a budget. They always made room for the poor in their hearts and in their checkbooks. Month after month, they made sure to send off a percentage of their income to local charities.

"God loves a cheerful giver," Robin told herself.

But as time passed, Robin felt detached from the regular donations she and her husband were making. "I don't feel any joy," Robin told herself one night as she wrote out a check to a ministry.

"Let's pray about it," Kevin suggested.

As they sat down at the kitchen table, they joined hands and prayed: "Show us how we can best serve the poor."

Within a few days, they learned of an older married team, Pat and Rick, who ran a food shelf out of their home.

"Can we come and see your ministry?" Robin asked as she talked with Rick on the phone.

"How about tomorrow night?" he replied.

"Kevin has to work, but I'll be there," Robin promised.

The following evening, Robin drove into the driveway of an older bungalow located in a low-income district. With the house brightly lit, Rick and Pat greeted her on the enclosed front porch.

After exchanging casual introductions, Robin looked around the porch. She noticed several shelving units stacked with shampoo, hairspray, and soap. On a nearby table, there were birthday supplies: colorful paper plates, a couple of boxed cakes.

"The food shelf is in the basement; this is the Supply Room," Rick explained.

"Supply Room?" Robin asked.

Rick told her that the porch area was reserved for supplies that might be suitable for birthday gifts. "The poor rarely have enough to survive; they can't afford birthday celebrations," Rick added.

Robin glanced at the scant supply on top of the table.

"We really don't have too many children's items," Pat said.

"What do you do when the cakes run out?" Robin asked.

Pat and Rick looked disheartened.

"We send the parents downstairs. We tell them to pick out their favorite box of cereal," Pat said softly.

Robin remembered the birthdays she had celebrated as a child; the decorations, the presents, the special way she felt when her family remembered her birth. It was hard to imagine a child receiving a bar of soap for a birthday gift.

As Robin drove home that night, she knew she wanted to be a part of this birthday outreach. *What can I do to help?* she wondered.

She began envisioning small bags filled with favors and candy and small toys. *The bags could be donated anonymously; the parents could give them to their children as a gift,* Robin thought.

Later that evening, Robin shared her idea with Kevin.

"It's a great idea, but how will we afford this project?" Kevin asked.

"We could use the money we've been sending to charities," Robin suggested.

The couple agreed that it would be a good way to serve the poor.

Over the next week, Robin and Kevin began shopping at budget department stores, filling their car with small games and cards and dolls and trucks. They also bought balloons and kazoos and small packets of M&Ms.

One Sunday afternoon, they packed and sealed twelve bags. Later that evening, Robin delivered them to the food shelf.

The next morning while Robin was at work, she received a phone call from the inner-city ministry; it was Pat.

"I have to share the most wonderful story," she said.

Pat explained that a young mother had arrived at the food shelf early that morning. She had ridden the bus to the ministry, hoping to find something for her child's birthday.

When she had seen that the boxed birthday cakes were gone, she had buried her head in her hands and cried.

"I prayed that God would help me." The mother sobbed with disappointment.

When Pat brought out the newly-donated birthday bags, the woman was overwhelmed with joy.

"This is so wonderful," the mother raved as she held a colorful bag filled with crayons and a coloring book and two kazoos.

As Robin hung up the phone, she couldn't stop grinning. It felt good to know that such a small contribution had made such a big difference.

The months passed and the young couple continued to donate the homemade bags, sometimes twenty or thirty a week.

They soon discovered that the need for their service was much greater than they first thought.

"The birthday bags always go very fast," Pat reported weekly.

Soon Robin and Kevin began exceeding their budget,

putting decorations and supplies on their charge card. They knew it was time to reevaluate their charitable giving.

"We've got to apply for nonprofit status," Kevin said.

When their application was approved, their nonprofit status enabled them to receive monetary grants from major corporations and bigger companies. The new status also enabled the couple to receive large product donations from local vendors and department stores.

The money kept coming. The products kept arriving at their front door. Soon their basement was filled with crates of crayons and lip gloss and chocolate candy bars.

Friends and family took note of the ever-expanding ministry. Soon an assembly line of volunteers agreed to decorate, pack, and deliver the bags.

Today the thriving birthday outreach is called Cheerful Givers. The charity now provides birthday bags to thousands of low income families in the twin cities area. Over 35,000 children have been served since 1994.

Each bag comes with a colorful tag that a parent can sign with a greeting of their choice. Though the tag seems insignificant, Robin and Kevin feel it is a way of restoring dignity to a parent who cannot provide for a birthday celebration.

Though the young couple has never seen a tag being signed or a bag being given, they often imagine the countless underprivileged children who benefit from their ministry.

Robin and Kevin believe that every life is worth celebrating and that God is pleased when a child's birth is proclaimed and affirmed.

Recently, Robin reflected on the many ways God has provided for their ministry needs. "It's hard to believe that giving to others could feel so good," she told her husband one night as she sat at the kitchen table.

Kevin just smiled. "God loves a cheerful giver," he said.

THIS PRESENT MOMENT

T he final draft for this book was due in a few days, and I hurried to complete one last story.

With the editorial demands of looming deadlines, I soon realized that there was little time to write a closing reflection about Deb, a coworker of my husband's, a young teacher and coach at the high school in our town.

Nonetheless, I felt compelled to meet this person I'd heard so much about. Leaving behind mounds of manuscript pages that covered my kitchen table, I met Deb for lunch at Coffeens.

While Donna served us the noontime special, chicken and wild rice soup, the two of us got acquainted at a table framed with sunlit windows.

"I love being a coach. The kids are great," Deb said. She was dressed in a maroon jacket monogrammed with the word "Coach."

Deb was petite, her dark hair wavy and short. She was animated; her hands waved when she talked and her eyes were like two small lights, bright and full of energy. She smiled as she reminisced about bus rides and basketball games and trophies her teams had won.

It was hard to believe that Deb was dying of cancer. At thirty-three, doctors had given her six months to live. She told me that a chemo pump was concealed beneath her jacket. "It's giving me a round-the-clock dose of medication," she explained.

"It's been hard for you," I said.

Deb nodded. I heard soft jazz playing from a CD player behind the counter.

"The disease is hard, but there's something much worse," she said.

I looked at her curiously.

"Holding unforgiveness in your heart; now that'll kill ya," she said emphatically.

Deb went on to share a story about a friend she had known for many years. Her eyes misted as she recalled an argument that had severed the relationship two years earlier, just a few months before she was diagnosed with cancer. Deb didn't give the details of the disagreement, only that she was deeply hurt by the words her friend had spoken.

"I spent many months resenting her. We didn't speak or call or write," Deb admitted.

When Deb learned she had cancer, she turned to God for comfort.

"I wanted God to fill me with hope and healing, but there was no room for God's grace in my heart, it was already jam-packed with hurt and hard feelings," Deb said.

Deb remembered the night she got down on her knees. "Please take away my resentments, help me to forgive," she prayed. In that reflective moment Deb's anger was transformed into unconditional love for her friend. In an instant, the heavy weight of bitterness was lifted from her. In time, she made peace with her friend.

"I felt so light." Deb laughed.

As she spoke I thought of my good friend Karen. The two of us hadn't spoken in weeks; an argument had injured our friendship. I had put off calling her, telling myself there would be time for reconciliation after the book was done.

"Call her tonight," Deb suggested. "Life is short," she reminded me.

Later that evening, I called Karen. "I've missed you," I told her.

"I've missed you too," she said. We laughed. We couldn't even remember what we had argued about.

"I feel so light," I told her, borrowing Deb's words.

That evening Karen and I talked on the phone, Deb was being admitted to the hospital for headaches. The doctors discovered the cancer had spread to her brain. Deb went into a coma and died two days later.

Her funeral was held in a large gathering space at the high school. She was buried in her coaching uniform. Over a thousand people crowded the service—teachers, students, friends, and family.

At the funeral many people spoke of Deb's optimism, her perpetual smile and her undying faith. As I listened to them share their thoughts, I was grateful for the brief moments Deb and I had spent together.

Deb had shown me that life is indeed very short and that harboring unforgiveness can hinder the miraculous power of grace. As in others before her, I saw an extraordinary God who is at work in the hearts of ordinary people.

On the back of Deb's funeral program was a poem entitled "One Fine Day." I'm told she had it posted on a bulletin board in her office.

As I come to the close of this book, it seems fitting that I should share it with you. This poem pays tribute to Deb and brings closure to the stories you have just read.

I leave you with this last reflection.

ONE FINE DAY

I may never see tomorrow; there's no written guarantee,

And things that happened yesterday belong to history.

I cannot predict the future, and I cannot change the past.

I have just the present moment; I must treat it as my last.

I must use this moment wisely for it soon will pass away,

And be lost to me forever as a part of yesterday.

I must exercise compassion, help the fallen to their feet.

Be a friend unto the friendless, make an empty life complete.

I must make this moment precious, for it will not come again.

And I can never be content with things that might have been,

Kind words I fail to say this day may ever be unsaid.

For I know not how short may be the path that lies ahead.

The unkind things I do today may never be undone,

And friendships that I fail to win may never be won.

I may not have another chance on bended knee to pray,

And thank God with humble heart for giving me this day.

I may never see tomorrow, but this moment is my own.

It's mine to use or cast aside; the choice is mine alone.

I have just this precious moment in the sunlight of today,

Where the dawning of tomorrow meets the dusk of yesterday.

AUTHOR UNKNOWN

ACKNOWLEDGMENTS

"In the Waiting Room," reprinted with permission from *Guideposts* magazine (March 1997). © 1997 by *Guideposts*, Carmel, New York 10512.

"The Divine Touch," reprinted with permission from *Guideposts* magazine (March 1996). © 1996 by *Guideposts*, Carmel, New York 10512.

"A Day for Heroes," reprinted with permission from *Guideposts* magazine (May 1999). © 1999 by *Guideposts*, Carmel, New York 10512.

"Drop Earrings" was originally titled "In Mrs. Lake's Eyes," reprinted with permission from *Guideposts* magazine (January 1997). © 1996 by *Guideposts*, Carmel, New York 10512.

"God Has a Plan for Your Baby," was originally titled "Homeroom Lesson," reprinted with permission from *Guideposts* magazine (June 1997). © 1997 by *Guideposts*, Carmel, New York 10512.

"The Truest of Friends," reprinted with permission from *Guideposts* magazine (February 1998). © 1998 by *Guideposts*, Carmel, New York 10512.